Not Just Wilberforce

Champions of Human Rights in Hull and East Yorkshire

essays for Amnesty International

Edited by Ekkehard Kopp and Cecile Oxaal

First published in 2014 by
Amnesty International UK
The Human Rights Action Centre
17-25 New Inn Yard
London EC2A 3EA
in association with
Hull Amnesty Group

ISBN: 978 1 873328 77 4

Design and typesetting by Kall Kwik Centre Hull, Centre 1292, The Woollen Warehouse, South Church Side, Hull HU1 1RR

Printed in Great Britain by Kall Kwik Centre Hull, Centre 1292, The Woollen Warehouse, South Church Side, Hull HU1 1RR

Foreword

This book is about freedom and Hull. Its contributors have all been variously embedded in the cultural, intellectual and political life of the city over many years: they know of what they speak.

Freedom — unlike poetry and prose — does not just happen anywhere. Indeed, it is the case that, although men may be born free, they are too often in chains. Freedom has to be won, sustained and protected. It is always at risk, the fact as well as the word.

The argument of this irresistible volume is that, as a city and area, Hull has a proud and distinctive history of resisting forms of oppression, of using an angular independence of thought to challenge the orthodox and of fighting for principles and practical change.

Why should this be so? The introduction suggests that it may have had something to do with Hull's relative isolation and the space it affords for thought. Today isolation is something of a fiction. Motorways, train connections, airports easily dispel the myth. But Douglas Dunn, a distinguished poet whose skills were honed in the city, makes a telling point: 'Like most cities built on the bank of an estuary, Hull has a marginal, provisional, almost frontier quality'. Being marginal allows untrammelled thinking; being provisional implies fluidity, flexibility and a refusal of fixed dogma; and being frontier suggests the pioneering spirit so obvious in Hull's past, the courage to go beyond.

So let us not pretend that Hull is geographically mainstream. It isn't and that is its glory.

As 2017 approaches, we need to revel in the city's difference and its hidden riches. In 1982, Genny Rahtz, another Hull-based poet, wrote:

So attend this subdued city
Providing for its livelihood
Not its looks,
And keep what you find secret
From all obliterating praise.

Whilst it is not difficult to understand this affectionate cradling of her workaday, unpretentious Hull, now is the time for the city to reveal its secrets. This book is a step out of the shadows — and the praise that it deserves to receive will not obliterate but confirm the area's uniqueness and will acknowledge its proud contribution over the centuries to the cause of freedom and all those universal ideals promoted so tirelessly by Amnesty International UK.

Graham Chesters
Chair, Hull Freedom Festival Board

Table of Contents

Introduction

Philip Larkin famously described Hull as 'a city that is in the world yet sufficiently on the edge of it to have a different resonance'; a place whose relative isolation, together with a turbulent, if less well-known, history, allows individuals space to form their own views, unencumbered by orthodoxy or distracted by fashion. His verdict, 'a place cannot produce poems: it can only not prevent them, and Hull is good at that. It neither impresses nor insists', is equally fitting as a description of factors that foster independence of thought and its expression in social and political action.

What we now call human rights have been wrested from the powers of church and state by the struggles of people all over the world. These human rights were codified in the United Nations Universal Declaration of Human Rights (1948). Its drafters drew on the main tenets of many religions and on secular philosophical discourses about what constitutes natural justice and freedom. Among those who fought for human rights were some whose words and deeds stood out in defining the aims of the struggle.

In any pantheon of champions of human rights, William Wilberforce is rightly treasured as a favourite son of Hull for his role in leading the long parliamentary campaign to abolish the slave trade more than 200 years ago. Arguably however, in the collective memory his fame has eclipsed that of others from Hull and East Yorkshire, whose writings and actions in the defence of human freedom and dignity deserve similar attention and local pride.

This small volume seeks to redress some of this imbalance by telling the stories of eight of these individuals (or families) with strong local connections. In their time their influence was felt well beyond these shores, and it deserves to be celebrated more widely than it is today. Our list is eclectic rather than exhaustive. It provides a representative sample that illustrates the freedom of spirit and action shown by people from or active in our region.

The lives of these individuals cover well over four centuries, during which British society was to undergo many fundamental changes, but clear threads can be traced throughout in the preoccupations of our human rights champions, and the religious or secular principles that inspired them.

Principled opposition to abuses of state power

John Walworth and *James Rochester,* two Carthusian monks imprisoned in the Hull Charterhouse in 1536, sought freedom to observe their religion (Catholicism) in the face of an Established Church forced upon them by Henry VIII;

John and *Matthew Alured* opposed abuses of royal power by Charles I, fighting in the English Civil Wars (1642-51) for a sovereign democratic Parliament, with Matthew turning on Oliver Cromwell whom, as Lord Protector, he saw as betraying that ideal;

Mary Wollstonecraft (1759-1797), insisted that democratic principles underpinning the French Revolution should lead to independence and social justice for women;

Thomas Peronnet Thompson and *George Cookman*, supporting the Great Reform Act of 1832, maintained that Parliament should establish fully universal suffrage;

Mary Murdoch (1864-1918), as Hull's first female GP, exposed health inequalities in the region, challenging neglect of the poor by the local health authorities of her time;

*Winifred Holtby (*1898-1935) opposed armed conflict and actively sought to promote world peace through the League of Nations and at pacifist rallies after World War I;

*Lillian Bilocca (*1929-1988) took on trawler owners and the Wilson Government in 1968 in a direct action campaign to highlight the owners' shameful neglect of trawlermen's safety and the poor working conditions on Hull trawlers.

Opposing slavery in all its forms

From 1800 onward, the abolitionist movement gained substantial impetus from

Thomas Peronnet Thompson, as Governor of Sierra Leone, in striving to improve conditions for freed slaves; later seeking to end the slave trade in the Persian Gulf;

the younger Cookmans (George Grimston and Alfred), both prominent in the drive to abolish slavery in the USA;

whilst parallels with slavery were rightly drawn by

Mary Wollstonecraft, arguing cogently that subjugation of women is a form of slavery;

Winifred Holtby, exposing the working conditions of black miners in South Africa as akin to slavery and fighting for an effective trade union;

Women's rights

Mary Wollstonecraft's advocacy of women's rights has greatly influenced progressive opinion for the past two centuries;

Thomas Peronnet Thompson consistently supported votes for women, despite it causing rifts with some former friends;

Mary Murdoch was a leading force in the suffragist movement throughout her life; its first major Parliamentary success came just two years after her death;

Winifred Holtby saw votes for women become a partial reality during her twenties and pressed for women's rights, mutual respect, peace and democracy all her life;

Lillian Bilocca's 1968 showed local women how effective women's collective direct action can be in mobilising public opinion against injustice.

Making a stand

While social and economic conditions changed beyond recognition between 1536 and 1968, all the human rights champions celebrated in this volume share personal characteristics that led them to make a stand for human dignity, justice and compassion wherever this was denied by the societies in which they lived.

Prominent among these are determination, courage, commitment and perseverance: our champions were not to be deterred from the actions they considered necessary to highlight injustice, irrespective of the personal danger or social rejection this might entail for them, nor were they discouraged by the setbacks and obstacles they encountered or by initial failure. Their actions were marked by selflessness, honesty and consistency. The firm principles underpinning their conduct were based on clear concepts of the primacy of human dignity, of personal liberty, of freedom of speech, of compassion for their fellows and of the power of reasoned argument.

The same principles underpin Amnesty International's robust defence of human rights wherever these are threatened: whether by despots, authoritarian or corrupt regimes, by discrimination and inequality, by xenophobia, tribal hatred and wilful ignorance, or by exploitation of the weak by the strong. In highlighting the words and deeds of past champions of human rights from our own region, we hope that these examples will encourage modern readers to remain vigilant and active in speaking out against injustice and in opposing oppression and exploitation in all its forms. Only if we value our common humanity, mutual understanding and compassion more highly than sectional interests can we hope to realise the ideals of these role models in building a more tolerant, compassionate, just and equal society.

Ekkehard Kopp and Cecile Oxaal (Editors), Hull, March 2014

Acknowledgements

This project was made possible by Councillor Colin Inglis, during whose tenure as Lord Mayor of Kingston upon Hull in 2011/12 Hull Amnesty Group was designated as one of the three local recipients of funds raised through the Lord Mayor's Charity Appeal. Our contributors generously provided their time and expertise and, despite vague instructions and tight deadlines, delivered their articles promptly. We are grateful to Professor Michael Turner (Appalachian State University, North Carolina) for his expert advice on the chapter about Thomas Perronet Thompson, to Kath Beal for providing valuable material on, as well as illustrations of, Thompson's life and career, and to Gertrud Aub-Buscher, who assisted us with copy-editing and valuable advice.

Thanks are due to Nicky Parker at Amnesty International UK for her help and advice and to Joy Gledhill of Kall Kwik (Hull) for handling the production of this volume with efficiency, patience and good humour. Every effort has been made to trace copyright holders of images used in this book. Copyright holders not credited are invited to get in touch with Hull Amnesty Group.

Note A version of this book (in soft-bound A4 format), funded from the Lord Mayor's Appeal, has been distributed to every secondary school in Hull and the East Riding, to stimulate local school pupils' interest in the fascinating history of their region.

Hull Amnesty Group

Meetings are held at 7 pm on the last Thursday of every month at the Zoo Cafe (off Newland Avenue, opposite Goddard Avenue). Everyone is welcome.

For information about the Group's activities contact:

anne@pmacnamara.karoo.co.uk, Tel. (01482) 445771.

For information about Amnesty International go to www.amnesty.org.uk, or write to

Amnesty International UK
The Human Rights Action Centre
17-25 New Inn Yard
London EC2 3EA
Tel +44 (0)20 7033 1777

White Rose is dead....

Patrick J Doyle

The Hull Charterhouse, with its neighbouring 'hospital', the Maison Dieu, founded by Michael de la Pole in 1384, stood amidst fields on the west bank of the River Hull, a short distance from the walled town of Kingston upon Hull. Michael's father, William de la Pole (d. 1366), a prominent wool merchant and moneylender to Edward III, was said to have been *'second to no other merchant of England'*. He had served as Chief Baron of the Exchequer and become the first Mayor of Kingston upon Hull in 1332. Michael, who also served as Lord Chancellor of England (1383-86) to Richard II, gained the title of 1st Earl of Suffolk (1385), having inherited the valuable East Anglian estates of his wife, Katherine Wingfield, ten years earlier.

Fig 1.1   Fig 1.2

Statues of William de la Pole (Victoria Pier, Hull) and Michael de la Pole (Guildhall, Hull)
By courtesy of Kingston upon Hull City Council

The de la Poles rose from the ranks of successful merchants to become princes, and their palace in Hull stood on the site of the former General Post Office, opposite St Mary's Church, in Lowgate. By the early sixteenth century the family had married into royalty: Elizabeth of York, sister of Edward IV and Richard III, wed John de la Pole, bearing him seven sons, cousins of Henry VIII. One son died young, two others took holy orders. The fates of the other four provide a stark summary of the family's rapid demise following the Wars of the Roses (1455-1487).

1

The eldest, John, had been named by Richard III as his successor, shortly before Richard's defeat at the Battle of Bosworth in 1485. John initially submitted to the victor, now crowned as Henry VII, but, in May 1487, fled to Ireland to join the 'Lambert Simnel Rebellion' (ostensibly supporting the claim to the throne by the young impostor Lambert Simnel), which was suppressed by Henry in 1487 at the Battle of East Stoke, near Newark, in which John lost his life.

John's brother Edmund succeeded him as Duke of Suffolk, but was demoted to Earl in 1493 and fled abroad in 1501. However, in 1506 he was handed over to Henry by the Holy Roman Emperor Maximilian I in return for the latter's son, Philip, who had been held prisoner by Henry VII. Despite Henry's promise to spare his life, Edmund was executed in 1513, early in the reign of Henry VIII.

Following Edmund's flight in 1501, his younger brother William was regarded by Henry VII as a threat to his throne and was imprisoned in the Tower from 1501, longer than anyone else, until his death in 1539.

Upon Edmund's death the youngest brother, Richard, who had also found sanctuary abroad, assumed the Suffolk title, remained abroad and, in his pursuit of the English crown, formed alliances with two successive French kings.
Thus the de la Pole family, despite their mercantile origins, were rightly considered by the Tudors as the real threat to their throne.

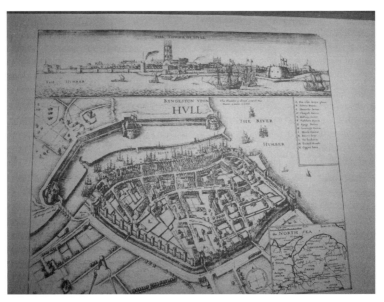

Fig 1.3

14th century drawing of the walled city of Hull, with Charterhouse at top middle, just outside the city walls. By courtesy of Rev Stephen Deas, Master of Hull Charterhouse.

The Hull Charterhouse (the English name for a Carthusian monastery) was initially established to house thirteen members of the Carthusian Order—an order of monks established by St Bruno in 1084—whose Rule (or constitution) emphasises silent contemplation. In 1525, while the Carthusians in Hull faithfully followed their Rule, at the Battle of Pavia, in Italy, the armies of the Holy Roman Emperor Charles V routed those of Francis I, the French king. This proved a fateful result both for the founding fathers of the Hull Charterhouse and eventually for the institution itself. One wonders what were the reactions in Hull to the news of the battle. In all probability they were very different from those of their monarch. Henry VIII was elated. After enquiring of the bearer of the news about the fate of the French King, he asked *'and Richard de la Pole?'* The reply came *'...the White Rose is dead in battle...I saw him dead with the others.'* To which Henry exclaimed: *'God have mercy on his soul, all the enemies of England are gone'*—adding, *'Give him* [the herald] *more wine.'*

One suspects the Carthusians would at least have said a De Profundis (a penitential psalm that is sung in commemoration of the dead) for Richard de la Pole, but his death dashed any hopes of a Hull-based royal dynasty, as from him and his brothers there was no issue.

However, this did not prevent Henry's continual purge of all Yorkists. As late as 1541 the aged Countess of Salisbury, widow of Richard Pole (a great-nephew of Richard III), was executed simply for being the mother of Cardinal Reginald Pole. Her son, initially a protégé of Henry, had refused to support the King's attempts to obtain an annulment of his marriage to Catherine of Aragon and to disinherit their daughter Mary. Their final break came when, from abroad, he sent Henry a lengthy treatise denouncing the 1534 Act of Parliament that had declared Henry as the only supreme *'head on earth of the Church of England'*.

The effects of the Battle of Pavia upon Italian politics were profound and made Charles V's influence supreme. Even in 1522 he had been able to secure the election of his former tutor, the Dutchman Adrian IV, to the papacy. In 1530 he became the last Emperor to be crowned by a pope. In these circumstances the possibility of any pope, even if he had wished to, declaring the marriage of the Emperor's aunt, Catherine of Aragon, to Henry VIII invalid was most unlikely, and the thought of his half-Spanish cousin, Mary, being declared a bastard, impossible.

Henry's response to his marital impasse was to have a devastating impact upon all monastic communities, including the Hull Charterhouse. Henry's break from Rome led progressively, under his Lord Chancellor, Thomas Cromwell, to the dissolution of over 800 monasteries between 1536 and 1540, their assets taken over by the Crown. Henry was opposed in various quarters, most notably in the 1536 Yorkshire uprising by the 'Pilgrims of Grace', led by Robert Aske (of Aughton near Selby). The uprising combined economic, political and religious grievances. Aske's forces occupied York, returning expelled monks and nuns to their Houses. The rebellion failed after Aske had trusted assurances from Henry's envoy, the Duke of Norfolk, that were never honoured. Aske, along with many rebels, was later executed.

3

The Carthusians were an austere Order, combining the lifestyle of a hermit with a mediaeval monastic Rule and liturgy. In England there were nine Houses, and they were held in the highest regard. At the Dissolution of the Monasteries, the Hull Charterhouse should, as a lesser monastery with an annual income below £200, have been abolished in 1536 but, significantly, it was spared on the petition of local notables. The Yorkshire Commissioners wrote to Cromwell that the Hull Carthusians were *'well favoured and commended by the honest men of Hull for their good living and great hospitality'*. This was only a brief respite. Although, under the influence of Archbishop Lee of York, the monks had submitted to Royal Supremacy and demonstrated neutrality during a siege of Hull by the Pilgrims of Grace, their House was suppressed in 1539, albeit not before one very significant event.

The London Charterhouse had refused to accept the King's claims. As Dom David Knowles so eloquently wrote, *'when bishops and theologians paltered [sic] or denied, they were not ashamed to confess the Son of Man. They died faithful witnesses to the Catholic teaching that Christ had built his Church upon a Rock.'* Two of the London monks, John Rochester and James Walworth, were sent to Hull, in effect under house arrest as prisoners of conscience, where they continued to deny Royal Supremacy.

Fig 1.4
Plaque at Hull Charterhouse commemorating the Carthusian martyrs.

From the Hull Charterhouse, Rochester naively wrote to the Duke of Norfolk, begging for an opportunity to address the King in person in order to demonstrate that Supremacy was against the laws of God, the Catholic Faith and the health of His Majesty's body and soul. The cynical Duke, busy in his double dealings with

4

Robert Aske and the other Pilgrim leaders, passed the note to Thomas Cromwell, commenting, *'I believe he is one of the most arrant traitors of all the others that I have heard of'*. Eventually, he made use of a court at York, which was dealing with the Pilgrims, to have the two London Carthusians executed.

The deaths of these men, temporarily resident in Hull, along with those of John Houghton, Prior of London, and other Carthusians confreres, sent shock waves throughout Catholic Europe. The wilful butchery of monks for their honestly held theological opinions by a Christian king lately honoured by a pope as a 'Defender of the Faith' (a title Henry had been awarded in 1521 for a pamphlet accusing Martin Luther of heresy) was unbelievable. The book *The Tudor Age*, by Dom David Knowles, has as its frontispiece a portrait of Houghton, by the Spanish artist Zurbarán, and this writer has seen in Granada a huge painting of the London Carthusians being dragged on hurdles to their place of execution.

Hull played a small part in this story, but an honourable one nevertheless. It echoes all the themes familiar to Amnesty International: persecution of refugees and exiles, purges, house arrest, betrayal, and summary execution. The stance taken by the monks in defence of religious freedom mirrors the courage shown by later defenders of basic human rights, religious and political tolerance and the defence of human dignity.

The story did not quite end with the upheavals of 1536-39. Henry's named successor, Edward VI, died, aged fifteen, in 1553, to be succeeded by Mary I, whom Henry had tried to disinherit. She married Philip I of Spain and sought to return England to the Church of Rome[1]. She restored a number of Carthusian monasteries, including the substantial property at Sheen, in what is now the borough of Richmond, Surrey. There a Hull Carthusian, Thomas Synderton, was active until 1558. In that year Mary was succeeded by her Protestant half-sister Elizabeth I, and Carthusian monasteries were once more suppressed. Synderton fled abroad, joining the Bruges Charterhouse. Another Hull Carthusian, William Remington, found refuge in Scotland at the Perth Charterhouse, although this, the only Carthusian house in Scotland, was also attacked in 1559. While John Bennet, with Hull connections, died as late as 1580 in the Roermond Charterhouse, in Holland, all signs are that, second time around, Hull men showed more resolve. For them, a 'white martyrdom' of asceticism and absorption in their religious life, instead of bloody execution.

The Hospital for the Aged survived the turmoil. Originally it had been built for 'bedesmen' and women – in effect, as a residential home for the elderly, who had a duty to pray for the eternal rest of the de la Pole family. In the reign of Edward VI responsibility for the hospital was transferred to the Corporation of Hull, and it survives to this day.

---

1   During her five-year reign some 280 Protestants were burnt at the stake for heresy, earning her the nickname 'Bloody Mary' among her opponents. (Ed)

Fig 1.5
Remnant of mediaeval Charterhouse wall

Fig 1.6
Hull Charterhouse entrance today

If you wish to visit a living Charterhouse, then travel to Parkminster, Sussex, the sole existing English Charterhouse. To view the unique topography of a Charterhouse with its individual cells and gardens, then journey to the site of Mount Grace, in North Yorkshire. For a tribute to these little-known martyrs, Rochester and Walworth, there is a blue plaque on the walls of the Hull Charterhouse. At least there the de la Pole legacy of a House of God where Hull's elderly can live and pray in tranquillity continues.

But the story of Rochester and Walworth has a very contemporary ring of honest men caught up in the whirlpool of what Harold Macmillan memorably called 'events'. For Hull it is also a story of what might have been, perhaps even a royal palace in Lowgate.

References

1. Chrimes, S.B., *Lancastrians, Yorkists and Henry VII*, Macmillan, 1964

2. Gillett, Edward, McMahon, Kenneth A., *The History of Hull*, OUP, 1980

3. Hoyle, R.W., *The Pilgrimage of Grace and the Politics of the 1530s*, OUP, 2001

4. Knowles, Dom David, *The Religious Orders of England,* Vol 3, The Tudor Age, CUP, 1959

5. Markham, John, (ed) *Seven Hundred Years of Catholic Life in Hull,* Highgate Publications, Beverley, 1999 - essays by Rev David Grant and Professor Barbara English

6. Scarisbrick, J.J., *Henry VIII,* Yale, 1968

Matthew Alured MP: Parliamentary soldier and radical republican champion of Parliament

Robb Robinson

The seventeenth century was a time of profound social, political and religious upheaval across Europe. There were many facets to the long-term instability that accompanied this process. One particularly crucial manifestation of the wider crisis on this side of the English Channel was the struggle between the monarchy and the Westminster parliament over the governance of the country. Parliament wished to curb what many of its supporters saw as the absolutist and authoritarian tendencies of the Stuart Kings. In the 1640s the resultant tensions erupted into a series of conflicts across the British Isles now commonly called the English Civil Wars.

The world, as the inhabitants of the British Isles then knew it, was turned upside down. Regions, towns, villages and even families were divided. Some of the soldiers and ordinary people who had fought against the Royalists or supported the cause of Parliament were radicalised and found a voice, most notably through the Levellers. By the standards of the age the Levellers were certainly political radicals: they called for, amongst other things, religious toleration, an extended franchise and a government or parliament answerable to the people[1]. Their ideas were certainly well ahead of their time and were said to have influenced many shades of later political opinion, but the Leveller cause was initially suppressed by Oliver Cromwell at the end of the 1640s.

In 1649 King Charles I was executed as a traitor and the House of Lords was abolished. A republican parliamentary Commonwealth was initially established, though Oliver Cromwell, as Lord Protector, later assumed many of the powers of a military dictator. After Cromwell's death, the monarchy was eventually restored with Charles II in 1660. However, an effective long-term process of resolving many of the underlying constitutional conflicts about the respective roles of monarch and parliament did not really get underway until after the overthrow of James II by William and Mary, in the so-called Glorious Revolution of 1688.

Though the subsequent political settlement brought about in 1688 did not lead to the resolution of all religious differences or to anything approaching the immediate creation of a democracy of all voters, it did lay the foundations of a constitutional monarchy, one where monarch and parliament governed in tandem. Much later, during the nineteenth and early twentieth centuries, under this constitutional

---

1   A number of prominent people from eastern Yorkshire supported or sympathised with the Levellers' demands. These included Major-General Robert Overton, whose family came from Easington, and Admiral John Lawson, born in Scarborough and also strongly associated with Hull.

monarchy, Parliament proved capable of being a conduit, a vehicle that could be used as a means of channelling wider demands for democratic reform. Thus it can be argued that it was out of this now distant seventeenth-century turmoil that our modern democratic constitutional monarchy eventually evolved.

Fig 2.1
Oliver Cromwell

Fig 2.2
'King Billy' statue, Lowgate, Hull (courtesy of Phil Haskins)

Kingston upon Hull was closely involved in so many aspects of these seventeenth-century struggles. It is well known that its citizens closed its gates to Charles I, a few months before the Civil War is generally considered to have started. Moreover, the statue of King William III on his golden horse, in the old Market Place, bears eloquent testimony to attitudes of many of Hull's townsfolk to the Glorious Revolution, an event celebrated for many years afterwards by a local public holiday known as Town Taking Day. This marked the day in 1688 that Hull opponents of James II rose up and imprisoned his town officials. A number of local Hull and East Yorkshire individuals, now largely forgotten, also played prominent roles in various aspects of these crises, none more so than Matthew Alured (1615-1694), a man who deserves much greater local and national recognition.

Matthew, like his elder brother John (1607-1651), certainly played a significant part in the political and constitutional controversies of the seventeenth century. A consistent champion of the rights of Parliament, his life spanned many of the most turbulent times outlined above and yet his substantial role has been comparatively neglected in a number of local and national narratives of this period. This chapter attempts to outline something of his life and place it within the wider seventeenth-century historical context.

Matthew was born in Sculcoates in 1615, just to the north of Hull's Town Walls, in the family home, a relatively extensive building which had been, before the Reformation, a religious house of the Carthusian Order, adjacent to the Old Charterhouse Hospital. Today, the Hull History Centre is built in part of what had been the Alured estate and gardens [4]. He was baptised in Sculcoates parish church, which once stood in the atmospheric old churchyard that still lies by the busy corner of Air Street and Bankside, now a small bush-green oasis in the heart of the River Hull's industrial corridor.

Fig 2.3
Part of Sculcoates churchyard today (photo by courtesy of Mike Park)

The Alured family were landowners, probably best classed as lesser gentry, and had settled in the Hull area during the sixteenth century. Thomas Alured, Matthew's great-grandfather, had been appointed paymaster of the Hull garrison and later became a Hull Customs Official. He became an MP and Mayor, and all subsequent generations of Matthew's forebears played their part in local, regional and national politics [8; p.7]. Matthew's grandfather, his uncle and his brother John also represented either Hull or neighbouring Hedon at one time or another [10]. The family had a long tradition of being on the radical edge of religious reform. For example, Thomas Alured, Matthew's uncle, was imprisoned in the Fleet Prison in 1620 for his opposition to the Spanish Catholic marriage plans then being proposed for the future King Charles I [5].

At the time Matthew Alured was growing up, Hull's future politician-poet, the young Andrew Marvell, was a neighbour. His father, Master of the Charterhouse, after being widowed, had married Matthew's aunt, Lucy Alured. Matthew's daughter Mary later married William Popple, Marvell's beloved nephew. There is evidence that Matthew Alured and Andrew Marvell remained lifelong friends despite their subsequently differing careers and political alignments [3; pp.383-385].

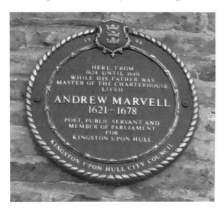

Fig 2.4
Marvell plaque at Charterhouse, Hull

Fig 2.5
Mulberry tree where young Marvell
is said to have composed his poems

When Matthew's father Henry died in 1628, his estate was largely inherited by John. A few months later, John entered Gray's Inn, London, and in 1640 was elected MP for his late uncle Thomas's Hedon constituency for the Short Parliament (which sat for only three weeks in April and May 1640, before being dissolved by Charles I). John was again elected as one of the town's two Members when the so-called Long

Parliament convened in November of the same year. By this time he had already established his radical credentials, having been reported to the Privy Council back in 1638 for declaring that the Scots 'would reform England by a Parliament as well as they have done theirs already.' He had been later released on a bond of £2,000 [7; p.151].

Matthew Alured made his entry into the festering national political controversies in 1642, the year he married Catherine Nelthorpe, when he joined with the Darleys and other Yorkshire families in petitioning for Charles I to return to Westminster and cease 'illegally' raising troops. During May of that year his brother John was also a member of the committee sent by the Long Parliament to Hull to assist the Governor, Sir John Hotham, following his refusal in April to allow King Charles to enter the town, an event that should rightly be regarded as the first overt act of the subsequent Civil War.

During the ensuing conflict John Alured saw a great deal of action. He was a colonel in the northern parliamentary army, under the command of Ferdinando Lord Fairfax. He fought at Adwalton Moor and is generally also believed to have been at Marston Moor, considered a turning point in the military struggle and, arguably, the largest battle ever fought on English soil. He was part of the group that Sir Thomas Fairfax took to London in February 1645 when he took up command of the New Model Army [10]. In early January 1649 he was appointed a commissioner for the trial of Charles I. He attended many meetings of the trial commission, including that of the 21st January when the verdict was announced. He was one of three East Riding people making up half of the Yorkshire commissioners who signed the King's death warrant [10; pp. 148-157]. John Alured was to escape the later fate of many other 'Regicides', as he died in 1651, possibly in military action in Scotland.

Meanwhile Matthew also made a name for himself as a parliamentary soldier. He began his army service as a Lieutenant of Horse in 1642, a few months before his first child Mary was christened at St Mary's, Hull, in January 1643 [3; p.384]. He took part in Sir Thomas Fairfax's attack on Wakefield in May 1643 and, although the attacking parliamentary forces were heavily outnumbered by the Royalist defenders, they overwhelmed their opponents. During the battle Matthew captured the Royalist army commander, Lieutenant General Sir George Goring [6; p.43]. Around 1,500 Royalist soldiers were taken prisoner in the action. A couple of months later Matthew saw action with his brother John when the Fairfaxes were defeated at Adwalton Moor. He was undoubtedly amongst those who fought skirmishes and a rearguard action as they fell back to Barton on Humber, from where the remaining parliamentary forces were ferried to Hull.

Hull had, of course, been besieged unsuccessfully by Charles I in 1642 after he had been refused entry to the town. During the second siege of Hull, carried out by the Royalist commander, Lord Newcastle, in 1643, Sir Thomas Fairfax, commander of the parliamentary forces, heavily fortified the town's defences. Part of their preparations involved opening the sluices and destroying parts of the Humber Bank in order to flood the surrounding area. This led to the destruction of the buildings of the Charterhouse complex, the family home of the Alureds, and the neighbouring hospital, which were razed to the ground to prevent the Royalists using them as a forward attacking position. During the subsequent siege the Royalists occupied the area around Sculcoates church, from where they bombarded the town. The Royalists stormed Hull's defences on 9th October, but the town held out and the defenders launched a counter-attack a couple of days later. On 12th October the Royalists finally abandoned the siege and Lord Newcastle withdrew his forces to York. The Alured family's losses in the siege were later recognised by the House of Commons, who agreed to pay John £5,000 in compensation. The Charterhouse hospital buildings were later rebuilt but the Alured family home was never reconstructed.

In 1644 Matthew became a colonel in Ferdinando Lord Fairfax's Northern Army. During this stage of his military career he fought at Marston Moor and various other actions before his regiment was disbanded in February 1646. During the so-called Second Civil War he commanded an East Riding Militia regiment, but rejoined the regular army in 1650 when he was made colonel of a foot regiment raised for Scottish service [11]. Cromwell invaded Scotland after the Scots had proclaimed Charles II as their King, and inflicted a substantial defeat on them at the Battle of Dunbar in September 1650. After a renewal of hostilities the following year, Matthew Alured and 800 of his men made an audacious night attack on Alyth, Perthshire, where the Scottish Committee of Estates–the country's erstwhile government–was meeting. The Scottish notables were defended by 3,000 Scottish troops, but Alured and his men seized almost the entire Committee, which effectively deprived the Scots of their central leadership. By January 1654 Matthew was military governor of Ayr, but a few months later he was sent to Ireland to bring a further 1,000 soldiers across to Scotland to help deal with the Royalist rising led by the Earl of Glencairn. Before these forces arrived at Lochaber, on the west coast, in June 1654 he had been relieved of his command by Cromwell and ordered to return to London [2].

Alured, who was a strong republican and supporter of Parliament, had become increasingly disillusioned with Cromwell and the policies he pursued. He seems to have profoundly disagreed with Cromwell's assumption of what was perceived as basically direct rule, under the title of Lord Protector, in December 1653. Cromwell's assumption of power followed on from the dispersal of the Rump Parliament in April 1653 and the dissolution of its successor, the so-called Barebones Parliament, later in the year.

Whilst Cromwell's popularity with much of the army gave him the power and support to carry this through, Matthew Alured, like a number of army officers and soldiers, having fought against one autocratic King, was dismayed. He regarded Cromwell's move as usurping parliamentary sovereignty, gathering power into the hands of one individual, who to him seemed a figure with increasingly authoritarian, even monarchical traits. His criticisms of the outlay on expensive clothing for the Cromwell family were reported to London and he was thereafter regarded as having 'evil intentions' towards the Cromwellian regime, hence his removal from command.

Whilst Alured had clearly fallen from Cromwellian grace by the summer of 1654, he was soon perceived as being at the centre of those disaffected with the Protectorate regime. In October of that year he was one of three colonels of the New Model Army who put their names to a petition denouncing the regime as contrary to parliamentary government. It was drawn up by the former Leveller, John Wildman, and signed by John Okey and Thomas Saunders as well as Alured.

Known to history as *The Petition of the Three Colonels* or *The Humble Petition of Several Colonels of the Army* and addressed to Cromwell, the petition demanded successive parliaments freely chosen by the people [12; p.21]. It deprecated the Lord Protector's complete control over a standing army, or as the petition puts it:

> *Power to be over such a Militia, as the late King durst not claim; that is to say, A standing Army, which may in a short tract of time...be made wholly Mercenary, and be made use of to destroy at his pleasure the being of Parliaments, and render...us and our Posterities under an absolute Tyranny and Vassalage.* [1; p.11].

Matthew and his fellow petitioners prayed:

> *That a full and truly free Parliament may without any imposition on their Judgements and Consciences, freely consider of those Fundamental Rights and Freedoms of the Commonwealth, that were the first Subject of this great contest, which God has decided on our side...and secure our dearly bought Freedome of our consciences, persons and estates, against all future attempts of Tyranny; and such a settlement will stand upon a Basis undoubtedly just by the Laws of God and man; and therefore more likely to continue to us and our posterities.* [1; p.14].

It is believed that the petition had circulated around several parts of the army and that those involved expected others to sign it, given rising hostility to the Protectorate. However, Cromwell's agents, having wind of the document, searched Alured's chambers and discovered the Petition. Alured was imprisoned in the Mews and the petition seized, but this was later published, most likely by Wildman [1; p.21].

The Petition of the Three Colonels, which emphasised the sovereignty of Parliament, was a challenge to the very foundations of the Protectorate and, as such, placed the colonels in real danger from Cromwell's regime. In the event, Alured, considered the most meddling, was cashiered for mutiny. He was imprisoned by order of Cromwell, initially for more than twelve months and then, after being allowed home for a period, was incarcerated for a further six months, this time at close quarters, and not allowed any communication with family and friends [1; p.2]. Okey was acquitted of treason and allowed his liberty after he surrendered his commission. Saunders seems never to have been imprisoned, but was also required to surrender his commission [12; p.33].

Oliver Cromwell died in September 1658, aged fifty-nine, and was succeeded as Lord Protector by his son Richard, who enjoyed no real power base amongst either the army or politicians [12; p.41]. He called a new Parliament, which assembled in January 1659.

Amongst those returned for the first time was Matthew Alured, as MP for Hedon. He lost little time in joining with other republican Mps to attack the Protectorate, as well as declaring strongly against the presence of royalists in the House. He supported the army's subsequent overthrow of Richard Cromwell's Protectorate and became identified as a defender of the sovereignty of parliament.

Matthew was appointed Captain of the Parliamentary Lifeguard and Colonel of Horse by the Rump Parliament [11]. Along with Colonels Okey and Saunders, he called for new elections and was a prominent supporter of the view that all standing forces and their commanders should be subordinate to Parliament.

In a period of extreme political instability, even by seventeenth-century standards, Alured, and others like him, were in a difficult position. He opposed the Protectorate but also the prospect of a return to a monarchy, and spoke passionately in support of the ideal of a republican parliament which had control over the army. His was a difficult course to steer in the tumultuous politics which the followed the fall of the Protectorate, and he seems to have lacked the talent for political survival possessed by his former neighbour and relative Andrew Marvell.

Further north, General Monck, for whom Alured had once fought in the Scottish campaigns, began to move his substantial forces south, intent on restoring order. Won over by Monck's assurances that he would preserve the republic, Matthew returned to Yorkshire in March 1660 to persuade his fellow republican and East Yorkshire friend, Major General Robert Overton, to relinquish the governorship of Hull. Matthew then stood as candidate for Hull in the subsequent parliamentary election but, together with Francis Thorpe, the other republican candidate, he finished bottom of the poll that saw his kinsman Andrew Marvell elected alongside John Ramsden.

During April, Monck also relieved Matthew of his command after some of his troops had declared for General John Lambert, a strong opponent of those wishing to bring back the monarchy. Monck did not maintain the republic and later that year was instrumental in facilitating the return of Charles II and the restoration of the monarchy. After the Restoration, Matthew Alured received a Royal Pardon, but lost many of the lands he had acquired during the 1640s and 1650s.

During the Restoration years Matthew was very much a political outsider and was briefly imprisoned twice in the early 1660s, on suspicion of being involved in plots against the throne. In 1673 he was debarred from taking the office of Mayor of Hedon for refusing to take the required oaths [11]. He spent much of his time in the East Riding, managing his remaining estates, which were scattered across the area, later residing in a house on the east side of Wednesday Market, Beverley. At the time of the Monmouth Rebellion in 1685 he and other 'disaffected and suspicious persons' were ordered to Hull to be searched [3; pp.383-385].

Matthew lived long enough to witness the fall of James II during the so-called Glorious Revolution of 1688, which gave us the basis of our modern constitutional monarchy. He certainly appears to have supported the overthrow of James II and the tenets of the Glorious Revolution settlement, with its guarantees for Parliament, and seems to have resumed some degree of public life, perhaps even office. He obtained a post with the Hull Customs, [9; p.196], previously held by earlier generations of his family. By then in his early seventies, he was one of the East Riding Commissioners appointed by Parliament to collect the taxes raised to cover King William III's costs for fighting first James II in Ireland and then the general war against France[2].

Matthew died in August 1694 and in his will he left the proceeds of his relatively modest estate, which included lands in Holme and Sculcoates, to his relatives and to the poor of the parish of St Mary, as well as to the non-conformist minister and the poor of the Presbyterian chapel in Lairgate, Beverley. He was buried, at his wishes, with little ostentation, in St Mary's Churchyard, Beverley [13].

Fig 2.6

Silver bowl (once gilded) with Matthew's coat of arms, gifted by him to Hedon Corporation in 1658 Reproduced by courtesy of Hedon Town Council

2   See for example, 'William and Mary, 1688: An Act for a Grant to Their Majestyes of an Ayd of Two shillings in the Pound for One Yeare. [Chapter I. Rot. Parl. pt. 2.]', Statutes of the Realm: volume 6: 1685-94 (1819), 104-142. URL:http://www.britishhistory.ac.uk/report.aspx?compid=46321&strquery=Alured, accessed 02 December 2013.

Today there is little physical evidence of Matthew Alured's life that can be easily seen. Two wine bowls, donated respectively by John and Matthew Alured, still form part of the Hedon Town Council Silver collection. The Charterhouse buildings of the hospital, which were alongside the Alured residence in Sculcoates, were rebuilt after the Civil War, but the elegant structures you will find on the site today date from the eighteenth century. The tiny churchyard where Matthew was baptised still remains, but no trace of his grave in St Mary's Churchyard, Beverley, can be identified. Colonel Matthew Alured's main legacy to us is not physical, in the sense of buildings or land. It lies in the story of his remarkable life and his enduring support for the principle of parliamentary sovereignty, held dear to this day.

References:

1. Alured, M., *The Case of Colonel Matthew Alured or a Short Account of his sufferings, by long Imprisonment, and the loss of his Regiments and Garrisons; for his faithfulness to Parliaments Cause and his Countrey* (London, 1659), 11.

2. Baker, H., *The Glencairn Rising, 1653-4* (Lancaster University, August 2005), 56 http://www.lancaster.ac.uk/fass/projects/newsbooks/Glencairn.pdf (accessed 1st December 2013)

3. Burdon P., Marvell and His Kindred, *Notes & Queries* 229, (1984), 383-385.

4. Gibson P., *A Personal History of Hull: A Brief History of the Hull History Centre,* http://www.paul-gibson.com/history/hull-history-centre.php , accessed 1st December, 2013. Also see Chapter 1 of this volume.

5. Healey, S., *Thomas Alured (bap. 1583, d.1638)* Oxford Dictionary of National Biography, 2004, online ed., Jan. 2008) http://www.oxforddnb.com/view/article/70628, accessed, 9 April 2013

6. Hooper, A., *Black Tom: Sir Thomas Fairfax and the English Revolution (2007),* 43.

7. Nuttall, W.L.F. The Yorkshire Commissioners Appointed for the Trial of King Charles I, *Yorkshire Archaeological Journal,* Vol. 43 (1971), 151.

8. Pink, W.D., Alured of the Charterhouse., Co. York, *Yorkshire Genealogist* (1988) 7.

9. Robbins, C., Absolute Liberty: The Life and Thought of William Popple, 1638-1708, *The William and Mary Quarterly*, Third Series, Vol. 24, No. 2 (Apr., 1967), 196.

10. Scott, D., *John Alured (bapt. 1607, d. 1651)* Oxford Dictionary of National Biography, 2004, online ed., Jan. 2008) [http://www.oxforddnb.com/view/article/37111, accessed 9 April 2013

11. Scott, D., *Alured Matthew (bap 1615 d. 1694),* Oxford Dictionary of National Biography (Oxford University Press, 2004, on-line edn. Jan. 2008). http://www.oxforddnb.com/view/article/66498, accessed 9 April 2013].

12. Taft, B., The Humble Petition of Several Colonels of the Army: Causes, Character and Results of Military Opposition to Cromwell's Protectorate,' in *The Huntington Library Quarterly*, Vol. 42. No.1 (Winter, 1978), 21.

13. Treasure House, Beverley, *Copy of will of Matthew Alured of Beverley esquire relating to property in Holme, Sutton and Sculcoates,* zDDX205/1 *24 Aug 1694.*

Mary Wollstonecraft: The Rights and Wrongs of Women.

Kathleen Lennon

Hull is well known as the home of William Wilberforce (1759-1833), who led the long and ultimately successful parliamentary campaign for the abolition of the slave trade. But East Yorkshire, this time Beverley, was also home, for many years, to the feminist philosopher Mary Wollstonecraft (1759-1797). Wollstonecraft, born in the same year as Wilberforce, campaigned against what she saw as another sort of slavery: the position of women. She claimed:

> *If women are excluded, without having a voice, from participation in the natural rights of mankind...man must...act like a tyrant.*

> *You force all women, by denying them civil and political rights, to remain in their families, groping in the dark...They may be convenient slaves but slavery will have its constant effects, degrading the master and the abject dependent.*

Mary Wollstonecraft spent her formative years in East Yorkshire (from the ages of nine to fifteen), longer than anywhere else in her life. It is said to be the only place she remembered with any affection. Initially, the family farmed at Walkington, outside Beverley, but three years later took a house in the town centre. She went to a day school that taught little more than reading and writing, which, together with basic arithmetic, music and dancing, was held to suffice for the education of gentlewomen of her time. However, she received useful schooling from Dr John Arden, philosopher father of her friend Jane Arden. He was a Fellow of the Royal Society, specialising in astronomy, and gave public lectures on science and literary subjects. Mary and Jane (who was educated at home) had first met at one of his lectures, and became firm friends, sharing a love of poetry and literature. The Arden family was poor, John Arden having been disinherited by his Catholic father for converting to Protestantism. Jane, six months older than Mary, was popular with her peers and aspired to become a governess.

Mary's father scorned the idea of female learning. The family's hopes were pinned on their first-born, her brother Ned, who was to train as a solicitor. Mary's autobiographical novel, *The Wrongs of Woman: Or, Maria,* published posthumously, reflects her bitterness towards Ned, in a fictional portrayal: *'a being privileged by nature—a boy, and the darling of my mother, he did not fail to act like an heir apparent.'* Fortunately, lessons from John Arden, who demonstrated a growing appreciation of her intellectual qualities, provided compensation for the neglect she suffered from

21

her own family during her adolescence.

A plaque on the house she lived in can be found on a house in Wednesday Market. For the rest of her life, in her letters, she referred fondly to walks on Beverley Westwood.

Fig 3.1
Mary Wollstonecraft

Fig 3.2
Plaque in Wednesday Market, Beverley

The Position of Women

Wollstonecraft's most famous book, *A Vindication of the Rights of Woman,* was published in 1792. It has recently been republished by Penguin, in the *Great Ideas* series, a series dedicated to republishing *'works of the great thinkers, pioneers, radicals and visionaries whose ideas shook civilisation and helped make us who we are'*. She is one of those.

At the time Wollstonecraft was writing, women were considered the property of their husbands and fathers (a position which led to the practice, still common today, in which a father walks his daughter down the aisle and gives her over to her husband in marriage, where she changes her surname from that of her father to that of her husband). In most cases they were unable to own property in their own right. Even in the social classes in which some education was offered to men, women gained no systematic education. They could play no part in political processes, either by voting or standing for office. To support themselves when they grew up, middle-class women needed to gain a husband. Jane Austen's classic novel *Pride and Prejudice*, first published in 1813, illustrates the difficulties women faced at that time. For without a husband, Wollstonecraft declares:

> *Girls who have been thus weakly educated, are often cruelly left by their parents without any provision; and, of course, are dependent on...the bounty of their brothers. These brothers are, to view the fairest side of the*

question, good sort of men, and give as a favour, what children of the same parents had an equal right to. In this...humiliating situation, a docile female may remain some time, with a tolerable degree of comfort. But, when the brother marries, a probable circumstance, from being considered as the mistress of the family, she is viewed with averted looks as an intruder, an unnecessary burden on the benevolence of the master of the house, and his new partner.

Who can recount the misery, which many unfortunate beings, whose minds and bodies are equally weak, suffer in such situations—unable to work, and ashamed to beg.

Concentrating on the position of such middle and upper-class women, Wollstonecraft paints a dismal picture of women who are brought up to be pleasing to men in order to gain a husband. They are preoccupied by their appearance and attractiveness; taught to make themselves docile and submissive, *'her mind left to rust'*. To aid her attractiveness the woman is taught to stress her physical and mental weakness, her need for a man to defend her:

Fragile in every sense of the word, they are obliged to look up to man for every comfort. In the most trifling danger they cling to their support... piteously demanding succour; and their natural protector extends his arm, or lifts up his voice, to guard the lovely trembler—from what? Perhaps the frown of an old cow, or the jump of a mouse.

Once a husband is gained she watches in alarm if her physical charms fade, for there is no other basis for her companionship. She is powerless when her husband takes mistresses or turns to prostitutes. There is a double standard of morality at work here. A woman's most important moral characteristic is seen to be chastity. She is an outcast from society if she takes lovers before or after marriage. But men are exempt from such judgements.

With respect to reputation, the attention is confined to a single virtue— chastity. If the honour of a woman, as it is absurdly called, is safe, she may neglect every social duty; nay, ruin her family by gaming and extravagance; yet still present a shameless front—for truly she is an honourable woman! But, in proportion as this regard for the reputation of chastity is prized by women, it is despised by men: and the two extremes are equally destructive.

Yet women brought up to think only of sentimentality, love and romance are particularly vulnerable to the attentions of seducers who, themselves unharmed by the liaison, leave the women as outcasts of society, often with children to raise outside of marriage. (Many novels throughout the 19th century are about this theme.)

> *Asylums and Magdalens[1] are not the proper remedies for these abuses. It is justice, not charity, that is wanting in the world!*

Working-class women were in a very different position at the time that Wollstonecraft was writing. They, like working-class men, had no access to education, but they worked in the factories, in the field, in domestic service. So although their living conditions were often very poor and they had many pregnancies to bear, they were spared the need to win men by vanities and the silliness and frivolity which she saw as following from this.

> *Many poor women maintain their children by the sweat of their brow, and keep together families that the vices of the fathers would have scattered abroad; but gentle-women are too indolent to be actively virtuous...Indeed, [there is much]...good sense which I have met with, among the poor women who have had few advantages of education, and yet have acted heroically.*

Revolutionary Times

Wollstonecraft was living in extraordinary times. The American Revolution (1775-1783), ending British rule in America, began when she was sixteen and ended when she was twenty-four. There were slave revolts in the Caribbean and America, while in Britain the movement for the abolition of slavery gathered pace. Most crucially, when she was thirty, the French Revolution broke out. On 14 July 1789 the Bastille,[2] in Paris, was stormed. Six weeks later the French Assembly accepted the *Declaration of the Rights of Man and the Citizen*, proclaiming *liberty, equality, fraternity*, and the right to resist oppression.

These events prompted fierce debates in English society. Edmund Burke, the pre-eminent Whig political theorist, wrote *Reflections on the Revolution in France*, published in 1790. It was a direct attack on the arguments for change voiced, among many, by Wollstonecraft's friend Richard Price. Burke insisted that monarchy, property and established religion must form the basis of the state. Wollstonecraft's fiercely argued rebuttal *A Vindication of the Rights of Men* (first published anonymously and then under her name) accused Burke of a *'moral antipathy to reason'* and ridiculed his demand for respect for tradition: *'We are to reverence the rust of antiquity'*. Her Enlightenment insistence on rationality (*'The exercise of our faculties is the great end'*), her commitment to human rights and an egalitarian, compassionate society,

---

1   Magdalens were religious hostels run for so-called 'fallen women'.

2   The Bastille was a fortress in Paris used as a state prison by the kings of France.

Fig 3.3
'The Storming of the Bastille on 14 July 1789' (Charles Thévenin ca 1793)

her contempt for Establishment values, were all given full rein. Hers was the first published response to Burke; it was followed by many others, establishing her reputation as an incisive, articulate social and political commentator.

A Vindication of the Rights of Woman followed in January 1792. Its initial spur was the proposal by Talleyrand[3] to the French Assembly for a new national education system that would provide state education for all boys–even for revolutionaries of the time 'rights of men' were confined to the male sex. Her rebuttal, demanding *'JUSTICE for one-half of the human race'*, written within three months and addressed directly to Talleyrand, was an excoriating critique of the society she observed, together with a passionate argument for fundamental change. Its publication was a sensation: it was widely read, translated into French and German and well reviewed; but within the year it fell prey to mounting panic in England about the impact of the increasingly violent revolution in France. Thomas Paine was indicted for his *Rights of Man* and, while her work was admired in radical circles[4], Mary's analysis of the position of women was attacked as 'indecent' by conservatives.

---

3   Talleyrand, Bishop of Autun, an aristocrat who had served under Louis XVI, but had become a prominent revolutionary, came to England in 1792 to win support for the revolution. He took tea with Mary Wollstonecraft in April - it was not a meeting of minds.
4   Mary mixed with thinkers known as dissenters, opposed to established religion and believing in freedom of conscience. Important figures for her were her publisher Joseph Johnson and the artist and writer Henry Fuseli, her first major love.

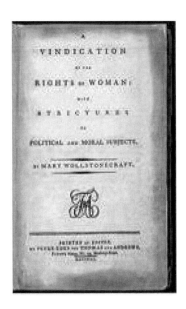

Fig 3.4
Cover page of 'A Vindication of the Rights of Woman'

Wollstonecraft urged French reformers, in their stress on liberty and equality, to remember the position of women. She did not support violence but was sympathetic to the overthrow of the monarchy. British writers, poets like the young Wordsworth, and intellectuals like Tom Paine and Thomas Christie went to France to experience the upheavals at first hand. Mary Wollstonecraft joined them in December 1792. Despite her opposition to the monarchy she was very shaken when she saw the king (Louis XVI) being driven through the street lined with guards, and later condemned to death. She stayed in France for two years, during times of acute violence (the 'Reign of Terror[5]') and often in personal danger, in the years following the revolution.

Reason and Enlightenment

In 1784 the philosopher Immanuel Kant had written:

---

5   The Reign of Terror (5 September 1793 – 28 July 1794) was a period of violence that occurred after the onset of the French Revolution, caused by conflict between rival political factions, the Girondins and the Jacobins, and marked by mass executions of "enemies of the revolution". Tens of thousands of people died.

Enlightenment is man's emergence from his self-imposed nonage. Nonage is the inability to use one's own understanding without another's guidance. This nonage is self-imposed if its cause lies not in lack of understanding but in indecision and lack of courage to use one's own mind without another's guidance. Dare to know! (Sapere aude.) "Have the courage to use your own understanding," is therefore the motto of the enlightenment.

He, along with many other thinkers of the time, stressed the importance to human beings of the capacity to reason. They thought the capacity to think for ourselves was what distinguished human beings from animals. *'Dare to think for yourself'* Kant argued. In stressing this capacity to reason, however, these thinkers privileged some human beings over others, namely educated white men! Women and African peoples, amongst others (for some writers working-class people in general), were not seen as having the same ability to reason, and were regarded like children, needing guidance.

Wollstonecraft believed in the importance of reason, in the importance of being taught to think for oneself. She insisted women too had this capacity, but due to their upbringing and social position they were not taught to develop and use it. In this way they became prey to foolish emotions and vanities. To develop this capacity for reason they must be educated in the same way that men were. (Here she is thinking of middle- and upper-class men, as at this time working-class men had little education). So in her book *A Vindication of the Rights of Women* she argued that both men and women were rational beings and should be treated as such. The French philosopher Rousseau had argued that educated women would lose their power over men. To this she replied, *'I do not wish them to have power over men, but over themselves'*.

She thought that many advantages would come from the education of women and by their being granted civil and political rights. They would be able to support themselves if this became necessary. They would be able to bring up their children in a much more enlightened way. They would be able to have friendship and companionship with their husbands, instead of the illusory relations of romantic love. They would be enabled to be just and honourable in their judgments about public affairs.

Would men but generously snap our chains, and be content with rational fellowship instead of slavish obedience, they would find us more observant daughters, more affectionate sisters, more faithful wives, more reasonable mothers—in a word, better citizens.

But men would also need to change. They would need to cease being tyrannical in their relations with women. They must be prepared to have respect and consideration for them; to honour those with whom they had sexual liaisons and take responsibility for their children. They must be prepared to enter into the affairs of the household, *'spend time in their nursery'*, give up their mistresses and treat their wives as friends and partners.

But unlike many of the Enlightenment philosophers, Wollstonecraft did not downplay the importance of emotions. She thought genuine emotions, deep feeling and a good heart to be important alongside reason. They should work together. What she criticised was the way women were brought up to be a prey to superficial and trivial feelings. With education and a training of reason, emotion too would deepen and be properly directed. She believed that *'understanding enlarges the heart'* and that *we should then love…with true affection, because we should learn to respect ourselves.*

She says, *'It is not against strong, persevering passions; but romantic wavering feelings that I wish to guard the female heart by exercising the understanding.'*

Personal Life

Mary Wollstonecraft was the second of seven children, four boys and three girls. She was closest to her youngest sister, Evarina. Their father, who had inherited a thriving silk-weaving business from his father, sold it in 1764 and sought success as a gentleman farmer throughout much of her childhood. He was not a good businessman and the family moved around a good deal as one venture after another failed. More seriously, he was a gambler and drinker and could be violent at home. In *Maria,* Mary later told of sleeping on the landing and shielding her mother from his blows.

Her father's financial ruin was complete when she turned nineteen; to help the family finances Mary left home to work as a paid companion. After returning to nurse her dying mother, she left home again to start a school. This got into financial difficulties, so she was forced to take a job as a governess, but she was soon encouraged by a friend to begin writing. Within two months she had produced her first book, *Thoughts on the Education of Daughters,* which the publisher Joseph Johnson instantly accepted. Written in the first person and based on her own experience, this text foreshadows themes she fleshed out in *A Vindication of the Rights of Women* six years later. At a time when educational texts took the primary reason for a girl's existence to be to obtain men's approval by softness, innocence (contrived if need be) and unthinking submissiveness, it was revolutionary.

From 1788, working closely with Johnson on his influential new journal *The Analytical Review*, she mixed regularly with radical thinkers, writers and political activists in London, and met her first serious love, the married Swiss-born artist and writer, Henry Fuseli. This relationship ended badly and, disappointed, she left for Paris, where, in April 1793, she began an affair with Gilbert Imlay (1754-1828). He was an American army captain, also a writer, and a businessman involved in land speculation. He had become a diplomat in France at this time. Although they did not marry formally, she regarded herself as his wife, took his surname, and believed this to be the serious, passionate and mutually respectful relation of which she had written.

She became pregnant and had a daughter, Fanny, while in France. However, Imlay's initial commitment to her proved to be only temporary and he left her. She followed him, first to Le Havre and then to London. With Fanny and her nursemaid she undertook arduous travels in Scandinavia on his behalf in 1795, which she described in *Letters Written during a Short Residence in Sweden, Norway and Denmark*. This book was published by Johnson in January 1796 and widely read and translated. But by October 1795 she was forced to accept that her relationship with Imlay was at an end. In her words, '*I leaned on a spear, that has pierced me to the heart*'. In her despair, she tried to kill herself by jumping off Putney Bridge into the Thames. She was saved by local boatmen.

Her life in London as an unmarried mother was difficult. Many of her previous friends and contacts rejected her. Although a controversial figure in London, she remained actively involved in radical discussion circles, where she gradually developed a relationship with the prominent author William Godwin[6]. A reserved, methodical bachelor, he was emotionally her opposite, but shared many of her political views, including her views about equality in the relations between men and women. They married on 29 March 1797. Godwin also took on responsibility for Fanny, whom he loved dearly. Sadly, following the birth of her second daughter, Mary died on 10 September. None of her own family attended her funeral.

Fanny, brought up by Godwin, was mild and affectionate but prone to depression, and committed suicide at twenty-two. Mary's second daughter, named after her, became Mary Shelley, wife of the poet Percy Bysshe Shelley, and was the author of the novel *Frankenstein*.

NOTES

A picture of the plaque in Wednesday market Beverley can be found here: http://www.hulldaily-mail.co.uk/Professor-visits-home-pioneering-feminist/story-18879675-detail/story.html

The quotes from Mary Wollstonecraft are from A Vindication of the Rights of Women; available free online at http://www.bartleby.com/144/103.html

The Penguin version is: Mary Wollstonecraft, 2004, Penguin Great Ideas: A Vindication of the Rights Of Woman

The quote from Kant is from his paper What is Enlightenment. This is also available free at http://www.columbia.edu/acis/ets/CCREAD/etscc/kant.html

A good, but not always flattering modern biography: Claire Tomalin, 2012 The Life and Death of Mary Wollstonecraft (Penguin)

6   William Godwin (3 March 1756 – 7 April 1836) combined journalism, political phi-losophy and creative writing. He was an early exponent of utilitarian philosophy, and the first modern anarchist. He is best known for two books published in quick succession: *An Enquiry Concerning Political Justice* is an attack on political institutions, and *Things as They Are; or, The Adventures of Caleb Williams*, the first mystery novel, is an attack on aristocratic privilege. A year after Mary's death he published a candid biography, *Memoirs of the Author of a Vindi-cation of the Rights of Woman*, which scandalised the conservative press.

Thomas Perronet Thompson: Governor, Abolitionist, Radical

Cecile Oxaal and Ekkehard Kopp

Thomas Perronet Thompson, the eldest son of Thomas and Philothea Thompson, was born in Hull on 15 March 1783. Thomas senior, a farmer's son from Swine, near Hull, was initially a clerk in the 'counting house' of Wilberforce and Smith, founded by the grandfather of the famous abolitionist. After the founder's death in 1788, Thompson became a partner in the firm–now re-named as Smiths and Thompson–and the family lived on its premises at what is now known as Wilberforce House in the old High Street. He worked with William Wilberforce in the campaign to abolish the slave trade and in 1807 became the first Methodist lay preacher to serve as a Member of Parliament. He campaigned for the abolition of the tithe system for tenant farmers, chaired the Hull Guardians of the Poor, initiated soup kitchens and used his influence and wealth to provide pauper families with land on which to settle and cultivate crops.

Fig 4.1

'Cottingham Castle', Thomas Thompson's residence, finished in 1816, which Perronet inherited in 1828. Let to tenants, it burnt down in 1869. The remains of the tower are in the grounds of Castle Hill Hospital.

Philothea Thompson's grandfather Vincent Perronet was an associate of John and Charles Wesley, the founders of Methodism. In the fashion of the day, the couple's eldest son was given his mother's family name and, to avoid confusion, we refer to him as Perronet throughout this account of his life. Despite his strict Methodist

31

upbringing, as a young man Perronet abandoned orthodox Christianity and became a Sabellian;[1] in later life he evinced respect for the institution of the Anglican church.

Fig 4.2
Thomas Perronet Thompson

Fig 4.3
Hull Grammar School

Education and Military Service

Perronet attended Hull Grammar School, then headed by Joseph Milner, whose brother Isaac, Dean of Queens' College, Cambridge, took a special interest when the boy joined Queens'. In 1802 Perronet graduated with first class honours in mathematics. His lasting fascination with mathematics would find expression in pamphlets on political economy, especially on the relationship between social justice and economics; his lifelong friend George Pryme, whom he met at Hull Grammar School, became the first Professor of Political Economy in Cambridge in 1816.

In 1804 Perronet was made a Fellow of Queens' College. Instead of pursuing an academic career he joined the Royal Navy as a midshipman and transferred to the army as Second Lieutenant in 1806. The Napoleonic Wars (1799-1815) with France resulted in land and sea battles ranging across Europe, North Africa and further afield. During a long military career Perronet gained repeated promotion, retiring from active service as Lieutenant-Colonel in 1829, and eventually attaining the rank of General. Under the Duke of Wellington's command he was awarded the Peninsular Medal for action in Portugal and Spain in 1813-14.

In 1807, during a failed expedition against the Spanish at Buenos Aires, Perronet was captured by the Spanish forces and released after a short confinement. On his return to England he visited William Wilberforce, who had led the long campaign by the influential group of evangelical social reformers known as 'The Clapham Sect' (or

1   Modalism or Sabellianism (named after the third-century theologian Sabellius) is the belief in a single God (opposed to a Trinity) who revealed himself in three distinct forms.

'The Saints') to outlaw the slave trade in Britain and its colonies, culminating in the Act for the Abolition of the Slave Trade in 1807. Wilberforce discussed Africa and the slave trade with his guest Perronet, who was

> ...so excited by the conversation that he sat up all night "combining arrangements ashore and afloat for opening or improving the communications with the interior of Africa" [2; p.26].

His resulting activities for the next two years form the focus of this chapter.

Crown Governor of Sierra Leone (1808-1810)

Fig 4.4
Modern map of Sierra Leone

Sierra Leone, on the coast of West Africa, had seen settlements of freed slaves since the late eighteenth century. In 1786 the abolitionist Granville Sharp, aided by charitable donations and the British government, organised the transportation of over 400 of the 'Black Poor' of London to land acquired in Sierra Leone, which Sharp grandly named Province of Freedom. These former slaves had come to England from the colonies and included some from America who had fought for the British during the American War of Independence. Others were unemployed seamen, acting as servants while waiting for their next berth. They were accompanied by some Europeans: artisans, women, a few teachers and doctors, and a sexton.

Sharp intended that the settlement, Granville Town, would be a model self-ruling one.

Sadly, it failed: many died from diseases; agricultural projects were unsuccessful; and the hostility of the native Africans, in part fomented by slave traders operating all around the settlement and within it—raiding it for slaves and inducing some of the settlers to become slavers—culminated in the native Africans' torching of the town two years later.

When Sharp heard that the settlement had been destroyed he asked the British government for help to restore it, but this was refused. Instead, he persuaded philanthropic investors to form the Sierra Leone Company, which was incorporated by Parliament in 1791. Significantly, this followed the failure of a Bill to abolish the slave trade. The Clapham Sect, inspired by Sharp's vision, saw Sierra Leone potentially as

> *an ideal society where races could mix on terms of equality, where free Africans would prosper by cultivation and legitimate trade, and the myths used to justify the slave trade would be finally demolished* [5: pp. 326-7].

The Act of Parliament gave the Company authority to retain land originally granted by the Crown and any other land it might acquire. Clause 5 of the Act stated:

> *It shall not be lawful for the said Company either directly or indirectly by itself or themselves or by Agents or Servants of the said Company...to deal or traffic in the buying or selling of Slaves.*

The directors of the Company required all the employees, *'under heavy penalty',* not to trade in slaves [2; p.28].

In 1792 another settlement, named Freetown, was established on the ruins of Granville Town. The British Government entrusted the management of Freetown to the elected directors of the Company, which was also allowed to make laws for those concerned in its affairs; in practice, the directors exercised the powers of the Secretary of State.

Sharp disagreed with these arrangements, finding it *'...repulsive to direct those he had intended should direct themselves'* and wanting a Company that would work mainly for the benefit of the settlers, not to make a profit for the investors [1; p.27]. Thereafter, he lost much of his influence. *'Thus a colony governed by absentees in England replaced the self-governing Province of Freedom'* [1; p.28]. Henry Thornton, a rich banker and close friend of Wilberforce, was elected to chair the Company by fellow directors, who put business before philanthropy.

The survivors of Granville Town (the 'Old Settlers') had attempted to rebuild their settlement at another site and kept the name Granville Town, but when they were attacked again by Native Africans they agree to be under the authority of the Company.

34

Fig 4.5
Freetown Harbour in the early nineteenth century

During the following fifteen years, two large groups of new settlers arrived in Freetown. The first were more ex-American slaves, mostly from the South, who had fought for the British during the American War of Independence and had been given their freedom and land in Nova Scotia and New Brunswick. Disillusioned with their poor farmland, discrimination and exploitation by employers, and finding the harsh winters unbearable, 1100 of them had come to Sierra Leone in the early 1790s, becoming known as 'Nova Scotians'. The British government paid the shipping costs and the Sierra Leone Company arranged the journeys.

The second group comprised Maroons, escaped slaves in Jamaica, who had formed separate communities in the mountains of that colony. They had been defeated in an uprising against British colonial rule and deported to Nova Scotia in 1795. Unaccustomed, like the ex-American slaves, to the harsh winters there, they asked to be sent to Africa. In 1800 the Sierra Leone Company arranged to re-settle 550 of them, with the costs of their transport borne by the British government. Upon arrival they were recruited to help put down an insurrection by the Nova Scotians, resulting in lasting distrust between these two groups.

All of these black settlers, as Fyfe notes, '...formed together a distinctive community of their own, neither wholly European nor wholly African', [1; p. 104].

While not expecting large profits, the Company spent generously in the hope that the settlement would be successful. However, it did not manage the settlement effectively. There was administrative confusion, in part because Parliament did not grant the Charter of Incorporation until 1800. Problems arose from incompetence, bad planning, poor organisation and dissatisfaction among employees because of low salaries, high prices and overwork. Those allowed to trade privately were buying and selling slaves, and crop failures on the infertile soil caused food shortages. Disputes with native inhabitants sprang up about the meaning of land ownership and the payment of tributes in exchange for land. There was distrust among the settler communities, and disagreements with the Company over grants of land. Adding to the difficulties were attacks on the town by the French. All these factors had contributed to the Nova Scotians' open rebellion in 1800.

Although the Company received increasing grants of money from the British government, the financial problems of running the settlement led Thornton to ask the government to take over its administration. Parliament authorised this in August 1807 and the formal transfer to British responsibility took place in Freetown on 1 January 1808, establishing the new Crown colony of Sierra Leone, thus ending the rule of the Sierra Leone Company.

Despite the transfer, the Clapham Sect retained great influence over the affairs of the colony. Indeed, in Thornton's view, they '...foresaw that the transfer, if it relieved them of responsibility, did not necessarily deprive them of power' [1; p.105], as Ministers who knew little about the colony would rely on those who did.

Perronet and Wilberforce had discussed the need for a suitable person to run the new colony. Wilberforce was so impressed by Perronet's courage, commitment and enthusiasm that he offered the young man the post. Perronet accepted; in the Narrative of Facts he recorded in 1811 about his Sierra Leone experiences, he wrote:

> Educated in the principles of hostility to the Slave Trade which the observations of every day have tended only to confirm, I had frequently viewed the transactions of the Colony of Sierra Leone with considerable interest, heightened by personal and hereditary respect for many of its principal supporters [3; UDTH 1/102].

Perronet would need all of the qualities Wilberforce saw in him in order to succeed in Sierra Leone. It was agreed that the annual salary of £1,500 would be increased to £2,000 when he took up his post. (With inflation this equates to well over £100,000 in current terms.) The high salary probably reflected the view that the posting was considered quite dangerous at the time, mainly because of the high death rate from tropical disease.

He landed in Freetown on 21 July 1808, after a two-month journey by sea. His instructions from the Secretary of State were to wait until the official communication arrived from the British government, in a few months' time, with orders for him to assume the governorship. Meanwhile, incumbent Governor Ludlam was to inform him about the affairs of the colony. Much to his surprise, a few days after his arrival, he found that Ludlam wanted him to assume office immediately, stating that he needed time to settle the accounts of the Sierra Leone Company. In his *Narrative of Facts,* Perronet explained that he had little option but to agree: the colony could not remain without a Governor, and Ludlam had authority to enact the transfer of power. Perronet was formally declared Governor on 26 July 1808.

Perronet undoubtedly went to Sierra Leone with principled determination and commitment. After all, the colony was intended to demonstrate that black people were capable of self-determination and not, as widely believed, fit only for slavery. A further pragmatic argument against the slave trade in Africa was that it led to increased tribal conflict, thus diminishing agricultural production and limiting opportunities for profitable trade with Africa through the exchange of British manufactured goods for tropical products.

While Perronet's direct responsibility was to the British government, he could not ignore the colony's humanitarian founders. He had also to take account of the African Institution, founded in 1807 by the directors of the former Company *'to stimulate trade in Africa, without itself trading'.* Headed by the Duke of Gloucester, its objects were stated as promoting the abolition of the slave trade, the moral and mental improvement of Africans and the dissemination of information about Africa. A former governor of Sierra Leone, Zachary Macaulay, was honorary secretary, and its committee featured eminent public figures: peers of the realm, bishops, senior politicians, social and moral reformers, including prominent 'Saints'. Perronet's father and brother were subscribers. All would be following his progress.

Nevertheless, Perronet had serious misgivings. Before he left England, Macaulay had mentioned to him a plan for *'redeeming'* natives (Perronet's underlining) and employing them in farming. Perronet suspected that the term meant a form of slavery, writing *'If I had heard an angel speak blasphemy, I should scarcely have been more astonished'* [3; UDTH 1/102]. During his voyage he was told by a former governor, William Dawes, that slavery had always existed and was necessary in the colony. Perronet concluded that *'all might not be quite right in this boasted Colony, & that it was possible for one face of things to be exhibited in England & a very different one in Africa'* [3; UDTH 1/102]. He resolved to form his own judgement at first hand.

When he arrived in Freetown there was a population of about 2,000 people, comprising: the various groups described earlier (including some inhabitants of mixed race); slaves whom the Royal Navy, patrolling the Atlantic, had 'recaptured' from slaving ships operating after the abolition of the slave trade in March 1807 and taken to Freetown, as the Act stipulated; employees of the Sierra Leone Company and their families; and slave traders and banished rebels who had taken advantage of a three-month amnesty after abolition to settle in the colony.

The task of governing the disparate groups in the colony must have been a very difficult one. Most of the population was black, but with many cultural differences born of their past experience in and adaptation to the countries from which they had come. Another consideration was the attitude of the ruling officials towards each group—'divide and rule' was a common strategy of colonial rulers. This practice was exemplified in an incident on the day of Perrronet's arrival.

As he stood with an official before the governor's house at the top of a hill, some Nova Scotians were formally introduced to him. Meanwhile, two Maroon chiefs waiting to pay their respects were sent away, without his knowledge, and told to return the next day. Perronet related:

> *The two chiefs of a high-spirited people to whom the Colony had several times been indebted for its preservation, one in his 83rd & the other in his 69th year had climbed a hill at noon in Africa to pay their respects to a young man of 25, while their tribe was waiting below to draw auguries from their reception—and this young man had been spirited away that the veterans might be sent back with dishonour to their people...*
>
> *The truth was there was a favourite race whom it was wished to introduce to me; for several of the Nova Scotia negroes were formally introduced to me...very respectable men, some of them, as I had afterwards occasion to know—but there was no occasion to insult the chiefs of a war-like tribe to whose fidelity the Colony owed its existence* [3; UDTH 1/102].

Somehow, Perronet quickly heard about this and ran after the two Chiefs.

> *"You are very young, Governor,"* one of them remarked.
> *"I see white heads to counsel me,"* Perronet replied.

He soon found further evidence of cultural difference among the inhabitants. Writing to Anne Elizabeth ('Nancy') Barker, his future wife, he observed:

> *There is much that is very doleful and some that is good. The state of European manners is bad beyond description. The black subjects are infinitely more orderly and decent. So much for this religious colony. And while the white inhabitants are roaring with strong drink at one end the Nova Scotians are roaring out hymns at the other'* [2; p.40]. In his *Narrative of Facts* he worries about the consequences of frequent drunkenness among officials, *'these reeling proselyters, these stammering & tottering emissaries of Christianity & civilisation among the acute & temperate Mohammedans by whom they were surrounded* [3; UDTH 1/102][2].

---

2   ...'the Protestant missionaries sent out from Europe proved totally unprepared for such a situation and incapable of working in the African climate. They quarrelled, fell ill, and one even became a slave trader'
[5; p. 328].

38

Even more serious for Perronet's governorship was that, as Sian Rees points out,

> *Slaving, still endemic across the borders, had been legal in the colony until 1807; however much its founders disapproved, it could not be expected that everyone would immediately renounce it* [4; p.24].

Rees suggests that Perronet was '...*simply bewildered by the diversity, the ingratitude* [of black settlers who enslaved others] *and the contradictions of the black.'*

But Perronet may also have recalled his spirited discussions with Wilberforce, the high ideals of the decades-long struggle for abolition and the hope for a better society in Africa. Now, driven by his abhorrence of slavery, he decided to use his powers as Governor to enforce the clause in the 1791 Act of Parliament incorporating the Sierra Leone Company, retained in the 1807 transfer of administration, which enjoined all the employees of the Company not to trade in slaves directly or indirectly, as well as the clause in the Abolition Act which dealt with recaptured slaves, referred to as Liberated Africans or Recaptives. The Abolition Act stated that

> ... *in no case should Liberated Africans be liable to be sold, disposed of, treated or dealt with as Slaves....His Majesty's officers* [were] *to enter and enlist the same, or any of them, into His Majesty's land or Sea Service, as Soldiers, Seamen, or Marines, or bind the same, or any of them, whether of full Age or not as Apprentices, for any term not exceeding Fourteen Years.*

Fig 4.6
Liberated Africans ('Recaptives') arriving in Sierra Leone - an 1835 drawing.

First of all, Perronet had to deal with the repercussions of an occurrence in March 1808, about five months before he assumed office, when two ships carrying slaves were captured. Some of the Recaptives were reserved for public works and the others were sold as 'apprentices' for a fourteen-year term. In reality, this was temporary (rather than lifelong) slavery: they did forced, unpaid labour, under threat of punishment. (The women were *'given away'*.) Failing to understand the subtle distinction between 'apprenticeship' and slavery, several Recaptives had run away, enticed by native Africans who offered them paid work. Perronet wrote to Nancy that some Recaptives had been brought back by the native Africans and jailed. There were disputes between the outgoing governor and the native Africans for the return of the missing public works apprentices, disputes which he, as the new governor, would inherit.

In the same letter to Nancy, he pointed out, with heavy sarcasm, that: *'...these apprenticeships have after sixteen years successful struggle at last introduced actual slavery into the colony.'* He was glad to be assuming office early

> *...because it will give me an opportunity of writing with more effect to Lord Castlereagh when in actual possession of the government. I am writing to Ld Ch and Mr Wilberforce very plainly about the colony, and shall assert roundly that if every step which has been taken in this affair of the apprentices is not retracted instantly the colony will soon be little better than a slave factory. The effect of this representation will either set the matter to rights or be very likely to whirl me from my government; but I am acting as every man of honesty and spirit would under the same persuasion* [2; pp.40-41].

When more Recaptives arrived, he searched for official papers that he was told had been received by the previous governor and found, *'among sundry musty papers'*, documents giving authority to hold a Vice-Admiralty Court for dealing with Recaptives. The Court was empowered to 'condemn' the captain of the slave ship, the recaptured slaves were to be forfeited to the Crown and the Royal Navy captors awarded a bounty for each Recaptive.

True to his principles, he acted. In front of a crowd he freed the jailed apprentices, told them they were free to work for wages and to appeal to him if they were treated badly. He promptly issued an official declaration that the sales and purchases, direct and indirect, of the above-mentioned slaves from the two ships be declared null and void and introduced an Act making it a crime to traffic in or keep slaves. He insisted that Government had a duty to ensure that every slave in the settlement had an equal right to claim the fair price of his labour.

Perronet made every effort to persuade the black inhabitants not to tolerate slavery and to ensure they knew of their right to freedom. In the *Sierra Leone Gazette* on 20 August 1808 he stated:

> *What African does not see that as long as a slave is permitted to breathe in this Colony neither he nor his children are in safety? What happens to one*

*black man today may happen to another tomorrow...you will act the good
and brave men; you will defend the Government which defends you; and
you will be happy...* [4; pp.23-24].

He explained to Nancy his efforts to make his intentions understood by all the black inhabitants:

[They] *had a natural jealousy of their personal freedom (for of political
freedom, whatever noise was made about it, they certainly had none at all),
this might perhaps be worked upon. I sent for their leading men; I went into
their houses and in the hearing of their families impressed upon them the
peril in which the personal freedom of every man of colour was placed if
the Acts of Parliament by which the holding of slaves was forbidden in the
Colony were in the slightest way infringed.*

*Why were men of colour considered as an inferior race? Because they
were black slaves, but not white ones. Could they ever expect to enjoy the
equality of rights which had been promised to them to induce them to settle,
if gangs of black men were to be seen working under the stick as slaves, as
at present; if they were to be allowed to be bought like cattle and transferred
like other property* [2; p.43]?

Among the important papers he unearthed, *'which might have lain there for ages
before they might have been found'* were instructions from the Privy Council. He told Nancy:

*There really is nothing which does precisely order us to apprentice the
natives of Africa, or prevent from using our discretion. I shall write to Mr.
Wilberforce and declare to him solemnly as a private friend, that I will never
apprentice a native of Africa, and that I will as soon take the rattan in my
hand and act as slave-driver upon the batteries, and that whenever I shall
find myself no longer able to avoid the apprenticing [of] the natives of Africa
I will instantly resign,* [2; p.45].

Writing to the directors of the Sierra Leone Company, Perronet made clear the
corruption of the apprenticeship system, relating one ruse he discovered on the day
he landed in the colony. A slave trader had suggested that if Perronet would allow
him to bring slaves into the colony and apprentice them for fourteen years, when
seven years had elapsed he would apprentice them again and by then *'they will
have pretty well worked themselves out'* [2; p.41]. This proved, said Perronet, that
new words such as 'redemption' and 'ransoming', which some employers used for
apprenticeship meant *'nothing but old slavery writ large'* [2; pp.41-42]. Unlike the

Company, he was not willing to wait for it to wither away as a result of the Abolition Act, the introduction of Christianity and education.

Initially, Perronet's room for manoeuvre to help the Recaptives was limited. Rees points out that London had provided no funds for their settlement. Although Perronet was able to place some children in a newly-founded charity school and provide land for the most competent workers, he was forced to allow the others to be 'apprenticed'.

But Perronet soon initiated schemes for employing Recaptives in clearing land, paying them low wages instead of bare maintenance as before, which

> *proved to be an effective incentive to harder work. The men cut their way into the woods 'with loud songs...they dispute the prize of vigour for their respective nations, and we advance into the country like a conflagration. Will slaves do this' [2; p.45]?*

He stressed the importance of farming, conducted crop experiments[3], offered generous land grants with security of tenure to those who cleared the land, so as to increase food production and road construction. His insistence that waged labour is more economical than forced labour did much to accomplish two of his main objectives for the colony: the eradication of slavery and the development of agriculture. Economic progress in the colony led two slave owners on the coast to offer to free 400 slaves, who would become free labourers in the colony, and Perronet could entertain hopes for the influx of capital previously deterred by the abolition of the slave trade.

A third objective of Perronet's was the defence and security of the colony. Although attached to the military for most of his adult life, he sought peaceful solutions to conflict. He faced the threat of imminent attack by an alliance of native chiefs who were slave traders and thought that, while their slave trading was being checked by the Abolition Act, some settlers still traded in slaves. Perronet sent messages to the chiefs to come and see that justice was being done about the slave trade. In the resulting treaty the chiefs agreed to defend any of their number who was attacked in his own country, negotiate in good faith in any disputes and elect a leader to command their joint forces in any conflict. Johnson describes this agreement as similar to the Covenant of the League of Nations.

However, Perronet's principled actions to put an end to slavery and what he saw as its many disguises, perpetrated by the agents of Company, fell foul of his superiors. When Lord Castlereagh received Perronet's letters condemning what he had found in Sierra Leone, he passed the letters on to Wilberforce and Thornton, and sent a curt reply to Perronet, ordering him to return to England. The whistleblower was fired. The directors of the Company, *'prominent public figures whose reputation and*

---

3   An experimental garden area outside the town was named Kingston-in-Africa in honour of his hometown.

attachment to good causes had placed them in the unique position of being advisers to government ministers and representatives of the national conscience' [5; p.339], feared that Perronet's disclosures would undermine their status and usefulness.

A letter signed by Thornton as chairman and dated October 1808, which Perronet did not receive until February 1809, sought to refute Perronet's claims. The key issue was the apprenticeship system. Responding to Perronet's accusation that slaves recaptured in March 1808 were sold like slaves, the directors wrote that they *'could not agree that the transaction ought to be confounded with that of a Sale of Slaves.'* They claimed that, since those slaves had been disposed of after control of the colony had been transferred to the British government, it was a matter for Ministers. Perronet later asserted that the directors' *'fatal error'* was to argue that, while Ludlam was wrong to make employers pay for recaptured slaves, their payments could be considered as *'premiums for apprenticeships'*–demonstrating their complicity in this scandal of surreptitious slavery.

Thornton had written privately to Perronet, challenging his proposal that the money employers had paid for apprentices should be returned to the employers. Wilberforce also wrote, arguing that acceptance of the apprenticeship system had been necessary to ensure the passage of the Abolition Act through Parliament and suggesting that, had Perronet faced the same situation, he might have done the same. Wilberforce added:

> *Remember that I shall always be glad to hear from you, and that I never wish you to use reserves in writing to me, though I recommend them in addressing bodies of men, or ministers...* [2; p.51-52].

Such caution had clearly been exercised by earlier Company appointees. Perronet discovered and published a letter from Macaulay to Perronet's predecessor advising him, as Fyfe puts it, *'to be careful what reports he sent home, not suppressing the truth but wording it carefully lest unfriendly readers misinterpret it'* [4] [1; p. 109-110].

Two months later Wilberforce penned another letter to Perronet, this time agreeing with *'the unanimous and clear Judgment and wish of so many Men of superior Understandings, Experience, Integrity, and Candour,'* and warning him to be careful in word and action to *'prevent public discredit.'* He was concerned about the impact on Perronet's parents, of whom he was very fond, and damage to Perronet's reputation.

Perronet was not daunted by his peremptory dismissal. By April 1809 he knew that the directors of the Company had advised the British government to recall him. During the months it took for the official letter to arrive in Sierra Leone, he redoubled

---

4   Fyfe comments: . 'By publishing this letter as an example of Jesuitical dishonesty Thompson started a cry that was to haunt Macaulay for another twenty years.' Thus Perronet's dismissal was at least in part the result of his refusal to be 'economical with the truth'.

his efforts to improve the colony. He wrote to Nancy, *'Since the news of going home I have manufactured the foundations of three new towns to their* [his enemies'] *exceeding great annoyance'* [2; p.54]. He also hoped that *'contrary winds'* would delay the ship bringing his successor, *'till our people get their land sowed.'* [5]

He worked tirelessly and did not escape contracting a 'fever'. During one bout he was dosed with so much calomel[6] that his front teeth fell out–the medicine made the patient salivate, to 'suck out' the fever. He never had the teeth replaced. Money meant no more to him than his personal appearance: his entire salary and some of his father's money was spent on the colony.

When told that his father had disowned him he said that for a man to be honest he has to act according to what he thinks is right, without *'waiting for instructions from parents or anyone else.'* And he meant what he said, in matters personal as well as political: ten months after his return to England, he and Nancy eloped from York in the dead of night and were married in London in March 1811. The elopement resulted from the refusal of their fathers to agree to the couple's engagement. It was a happy and successful union, producing six children.

After his return to England in May 1810 Perronet demanded a full public inquiry into his recall, as well as his salary for his time at sea, which with his customary mathematical application he calculated to be £392 14s 11 1/4d. No inquiry was held, and he was told that his dismissal meant that he would not be paid. A futile meeting with Wilberforce, including his former mentor Isaac Milner, led to a final break. Wilberforce would neither discuss his protege's actions in Sierra Leone nor countenance Perronet's suggestion of a debate in the House of Commons about whether the Abolition Act had not resulted in a new form of slavery.

Perronet commented bitterly to Nancy that *'Mr W. has thought that* a little *slavery might be connived at,* a little breaking of a few Acts of Parliament, *so long as the slaves were made good Christians in return for it, and* that *has been the Delilah that seduced him...Yet I view him not with malice, but with more pity than it were perhaps good for him to know'* [5; p. 348].

His father, torn between his son's desire for support in the controversy and his long and close friendship with Wilberforce, decided that he disapproved of Perronet's actions and would not help. This meant that he had hardly enough money to live on, especially with a wife to support. Nancy returned to her parents for the birth of their first child, and Perronet wrote to a friend that *'I shall actually have to appeal to my Father to clear me of some small debts instead of living on my savings'* [2; p.67]. A cousin of Perronet's intervened by sending Mrs Thompson copies of

5   Fate granted his wish: his successor's arrival was delayed by ten months until February 1810; time well used by Perronet to improve living conditions in the colony.

6   Calomel, or mercury(l) chloride, a dense yellowish-white compound, was widely used as an internal medicine or laxative in the early nineteenth century, making patients salivate to 'release impurities'.

(presumably) complimentary addresses to Perronet which he had received from important inhabitants of Sierra Leone. Soon afterwards Perronet was given a half-yearly allowance from his father [2; p.71].

He returned to Queens' College to write his *Narrative of Facts* to vindicate his governorship. He rigorously defended his actions and attacked scathingly what he saw as the corruption of some of the employees of the Company and, in their communications with the directors in London, their misrepresentation of what they were doing.

Vindication of the policies of his governorship came much later, in the light of subsequent events in Sierra Leone, the most deplorable of which was that the slave trade he had so determinedly tried to stamp out continued into the 1830s. Had the British government supported him, thousands would have been saved from slavery. Also, as Turner writes in [5], Perronet's policies on economic development–on the importance of agriculture, the settlement of freed slaves to farm the land, land grants with security of tenure, and trade–were later implemented. His peace treaties with tribal chiefs were followed up, but: '*...the debate about the best labour system for Britain's African colonies, to which Thompson had made significant contributions, went on through the nineteenth century, for the concerns which had vexed him in 1808-1810 did not disappear.*'

Perronet left a lasting impression on former slaves in Sierra Leone; in October 1830 some Jamaican ex-slaves sought his help with a petition to Queen Victoria for their return to Jamaica. Even in the 1860s he was still contributing letters to *The Anti-Slavery Reporter*.

Two pithy assessments, made much later, sum up Perronet's governorship: he was '*more vigorous than was pleasing to the Home Government in putting down the slave trade*' (obituary, Leeds Mercury, 9 September 1869) and '*too intellectual and scrupulous to make a good colonial administrator*'[7]. Vigorous, intellectual and scrupulous, he was also courageous, far-sighted and resolute in a great cause, in the face of powerful interests, family ties and the loss of influential friends.

In 1979 Hull twinned with Freetown. The stated purpose of the twinning is to promote friendship and understanding between the cities of Kingston upon Hull and Freetown; strengthen commercial, educational and cultural links between the two cities and stimulate and foster mutual exchanges at all levels between the peoples of the two cities. These are ideals that Perronet would have endorsed wholeheartedly.

---

7   AP Kup, Sir Charles MacCarthy (1768-1824), Soldier and Administrator, International Journal of African Historical Studies v(ii) (1972), 203-220.

Life after Sierra Leone

Like a true polymath, Perronet had many varied, passionate interests, leaving his mark in diverse spheres. He returned to active military duty in October 1812, served in the Peninsular campaign, and was then sent to Bombay in 1815 as interpreter and adviser to the army. He learnt Arabic and when a treaty was drawn up in 1820 between the United Kingdom and the chieftains in the Persian Gulf, he insisted on a clause forbidding the slave trade in the area, terming it plunder and piracy.

Back in London early in 1823, Perronet quickly became involved in political writing, which was to remain a consuming passion. Through his close friendship with John Bowring[8] he contributed to the influential journal *The Westminster Review*[9], joining the Radical philosophers headed by Jeremy Bentham (whose *Leading Principles* Perronet translated into Arabic). His opposition to slavery was unremitting. He used the *Westminster Review* (No. XI, October 1829, p. 275) to express indignation that *'the colonists have tried to frighten the government and the country, by holding out the necessity that, in the event of the emancipation of their slaves they should be paid for them; and some of the friends of emancipation have been weak enough to show an inclination to admit the principle.'*

In an excoriating refutation of claims of the inferiority of black people, in a book by an American writer, Perronet predicted that there would never be any good for the Americans until they have a black President, and that *'it may be sooner than some people think'*, (*Westminster Review*, No. XX, January 1834, p. 177).

He became an influential commentator in the *Review,* defining political economy succinctly as *'the art of preventing ourselves from being plundered by our betters'*. He published several articles as pamphlets (anonymously, while a serving soldier): *The True Theory of Rent* (using his mathematical training to argue–in opposition to Ricardo and Mill–that demand for agricultural produce, rather than production costs, determined the level of rent for tenant farmers) and *Catechism of the Corn Laws* (espousing free international trade, which had been badly affected by the Napoleonic Wars; opposing landowners' insistence on the imposition of duties on imported corn, and the resulting high price of bread). Both aroused much discussion, including debates in Parliament - but the Corn Laws were only repealed after the Irish potato famine.

Perronet became wealthy upon inheriting his father's estate in 1828 and withdrew

---

8   Bowring was a political economist, friend of and sometime secretary to Jeremy Bentham, traveller, miscellaneous writer, polyglot, and the 4th Governor of Hong Kong. He and Perronet shared 'a commitment to the cause of liberty abroad' [6; para. 5], working together in support of Greek independence from the Ottoman Empire and to re-establish personal freedom in Spain.

9   Established by Bentham and James Mill in 1824 this was the principal quarterly of the Philosophical Radicals, whose contributors included Byron, Coleridge, John Stuart Mill and Thomas Carlyle.

from active military service to devote himself to political journalism. He purchased a half-share of the *Westminster Review*, Bentham retaining the remaining half, with Bowring and Perronet designated as joint editors. In practice Perronet did most of the work. During the six years of his part-ownership he was the *'life and soul'* [2] of the *Review*, contributing articles to each issue on topics such as Catholic Emancipation (reprinted as the widely read pamphlet *'Catholic State Waggon'*), slavery in the West Indies, the cause of the Jews in England, and further attacks on the Corn Laws. In January 1830, in *Radical Reform* (later a pamphlet) he declared that *'the middle classes will use the legitimate power they have to obtain the legitimate power they have not'*, an ambition only partially realised by the extension of suffrage to middle-class property owners in the Great Reform Act of 1832.

Perronet was well aware of the limitations of the Act and continued throughout his life to press for universal suffrage, which for him manifestly included votes for women. His insistence on the case for women's suffrage later caused a rift with Bowring. Campaigns for women's suffrage gained momentum only in the 1860s, his final decade, but its proponents were well aware of their debt to Perronet. In a lecture delivered on 24 February 1869 to the Clifton and Bristol Society for Women's Suffrage, Prof F. W. Newman approvingly quotes the *'plain-spoken statesman of vigorous and original thought'* Perronet Thompson, writing in 1841:

> *Half the follies, half the brutalities, committed by nations, and for which they have paid the price in long arrears of punishment and suffering, would have been prevented, if they had been presented to the ordeal of the right-minded and clear-headed Women of the land. When real necessities occur to nations, Women have never been found deficient in the virtues which such times demand.*

Having disdained a parliamentary career (when his friend George Pryme was elected in 1833, he wrote that he was *'rejoicing daily at having escaped from that temptation of the enemy'*, [2]), Perronet changed his mind a year later, when the King had formed *'an administration of the opponents of the Reform Bill'*. He sold the *Westminster Review*, stood unsuccessfully as a candidate in Preston, but won a by-election in Hull in 1835 by five votes, surviving a petition (costly to both sides) to the House by the defeated Tory candidate. Rather than contest the seat again in 1837, Perronet stood in Maidstone instead, where he lost to the young Benjamin Disraeli. It would be a further ten years before Perronet was again elected to Parliament, although he contested several elections during that period. In 1847 he entered Parliament as the Member for Bradford, serving until 1852, and again in 1857-59.

Assiduous in informing his constituents, he sent letters twice weekly for publication in friendly local newspapers (the *Hull Advertiser* and *Hull Rockingham*). His unwavering emphasis on the repeal of the Corn Laws led to clashes with less single-minded Liberal and Radical MPs. He supported the aim of William Lovett's London Working Men's Association to establish *'Universal suffrage, equal representation, free election of representatives without reference to property, the* [secret] *Ballot and short Parliaments of fixed duration, the limit not to exceed three years'* [1]— ambitions repeated in the People's Charter of May 1838.

Nonetheless, by 1837 he had neither his Parliamentary seat nor the *Review*. His closest associates were Lovett's Chartists, although Perronet added repeal of the Corn Laws, *'total freedom of the Press'* and the demand for *'a secular system of education'* to the causes he espoused. His frustrating decade in the political wilderness was dominated by his work for the Anti-Corn Law League, which he struggled to reconcile with the Chartists. With repeal of the Corn Laws finally taking effect on 1 February 1849, Perronet was hailed as the 'Buonaparte of the Corn Laws'. He continued his practice of involving his constituents; yet never learned the *'art of commanding the attention of his fellow M.P.s'* [1]. His speeches outside the House and his pamphlets, such as *'Catechism on the Currency'* (advocating the gold standard) and *'Catechism on the* [Secret] *Ballot'*, were more influential and widely read.

Perronet's experiences in Sierra Leone, India and the Persian Gulf convinced him that, while accepting the reality of empire, *'the imperial relationship should not be one-sided. It had to rest on mutual benefits, not coercion and exploitation'* [6; para 7]. Unlike his contemporaries he did not believe in a natural hierarchy of races, and demanded respect for the rights and customs of native peoples in the colonies. In response to the Maori wars in New Zealand in the 1840s he attacked the government for reneging on previous pledges to the Maoris, and argued (in vain) for negotiation and rapprochement rather than enduring conflict.

After the Indian Mutiny of 1857, which was rooted in the colonial administration's insensitive attitudes to Hinduism and Islam (the local Sepoy troops refused to touch rifle cartridges greased with cow or pig fat, were disciplined, rebelled violently and were then brutally suppressed), Perronet became the Indian soldiers' main parliamentary advocate. He argued that *the most important part of the question, the breach of military faith and honour with the soldiers of the Native Indian Army* had been ignored in the government's response. As he elaborated in further speeches and articles (published as the influential text *Audi Alteram Partem*—Hear the Other Side), the promise to the troops upon enlistment, that there would be no interference with their religious practices, had been broken. The Mutiny hardened racist opinions in Britain and Perronet was shouted down in Parliament, while the Indians rightly regarded him as their champion against injustice.

Radical politics consumed the bulk of Perronet's energies, yet his restless mind found much else to occupy him: natural history fascinated him from a young age, an interest initially nurtured by his family's man-servant (a Methodist class-leader), who *'taught him the names and habits of beasts and birds and plants'* [2; p.4]. In Sierra Leone he found himself daily *'compelled to see objects of natural curiosity'* and he told Nancy that *'A letter would be run off in the presence of two 'alligators'* (crocodiles?) *in a tub, four snakes, two lizards* (iguana) *and an otter which had been bitten by one of the alligators'* [2; p.55]. Similarly, India aroused his scientific curiosity,

with *'elephants, tigers, lions, bears, birds with tails, birds without tails'* [2; p.19].
His academic training led to an abiding interest in the mathematical aspects of
musical harmony. In 1829 he published *'Instructions to my daughter for playing on the
Enharmonic guitar'*; by 1834 this had led to the construction of an enharmonic organ
with 40 notes to the octave, described in detail in the *Review* in 1835. Perronet's
invention was featured in the Great Exhibition of 1851. He composed a letter to his
daughter on the subject in the morning before he died, aged 86, on 6 September
1869, in London. He is buried in Kensal Green Cemetery.

References

1. Fyfe, C., *A History of Sierra Leone*, Oxford University Press, 1962

2. Johnson, L.G., *General T. Perronet Thompson*, George Allen & Unwin, London, 1957

3. Papers of Thomas Perronet Thompson (1783-1869); *Hull University Archives*, Hull History
Centre, http://www.hull.ac.uk/arc/downloads/DTHcatalogue.pdf

4. Rees, S., *Sweet Water and Bitter. The Ships that stopped the Slave Trade,* Chatto & Windus,
London, 2009.

5. Turner, M.J., The limits of Abolition: Government, Saints and the 'African Question', c.1780-
1820, *The English Historical Review*, Vol. 112, No. 446, (1997), 319-357.

6. Turner, M.J. *'Raising up Dark Englishmen'* Thomas Perronet Thompson, Colonies, Race and
the Indian Mutiny, *Journal of Colonialism and Colonial History*, 6:1, (2005), www.muse.jhu.edu.

Three Generations of Cookmans: a story of liberty and anti-slavery in Hull and The United States

Robb Robinson

In the nineteenth century three generations of the Cookman family made a remarkable contribution to the cause of liberty, in the fields of emancipation, political reform and spiritual revival on both sides of the Atlantic. Their story begins with George Cookman in the East Riding of Yorkshire.

George was born in 1774 at North Cliff Farm, in the parish of Owthorne, in the East Riding of Yorkshire. Both the farm where he was born and St Peter's, the cliff-top parish church where he was baptised, have since been swept away by the fast eroding sea [2; p.1]. Around 1788, when he was thirteen years old, he left home to take up a leather finishing apprenticeship in Hull.

In 1793, whilst still an apprentice, he became a member of the Wesleyan Society, having apparently been profoundly influenced by Joseph Benson, regarded as one of John Wesley's foremost preachers, and remained a Methodist for the rest of his life. In 1796 he became a local preacher and for much of the following thirty-three years he rode on horseback around a thirty-mile preaching circuit every Sunday [3; p.20]. George also played a part in the formation of the 'Poor and Stranger's Friend Society' in Hull, described as a gathering of a *'few serious persons united for visiting the poor and distressed, making them acquainted with their best interests, ministering to their bodily wants'* [5; 11 Feb 1797]. Both men and women from the Society, which was active throughout much of the first half of the nineteenth century, visited the homes of those in need around the town.

After completing his indentures George seems soon to have gone into business on his own and subsequently built up a substantial leather finishing company with premises off Anlaby Road. In July 1799 he married Mary Chambers, from Halsham, also an ardent Methodist, in Hull's Holy Trinity Church. The first of their three children, christened George Grimston, was born in November 1800.

George was more than a successful Methodist businessman; he became known for his strong political views. He and his young family were noted for their strong opposition to slavery and their support for William Wilberforce and the anti-slavery movement. But George was far more radical than Wilberforce in his overall political outlook, being described by his eldest son, at a later date, as being *'independent in his feelings, even to the verge of republicanism'* [8; p.2]. Such radical views found little favour amongst the political establishment in the repressive post-Napoleonic period. But political pressures for change, which built up during the later 1820s, eventually led to the passage of the Great Reform Act, enfranchising male middle-class householders. Typically for George, this did not go far enough and he later expressed on a number of occasions his disappointment that more people were not enfranchised by the 1832 Act.

He was also disappointed that the requirement for a secret ballot was not included in the legislation and in fact did not become law until 1872 [2; p.68],[6; 3 Dec 1839]. Nevertheless, after the passage of the Great Reform Act, George was soon in a position to put some of his political ideas into practice. The subsequent passage of the 1834 Municipal Corporations Act led ultimately to the end of the old Hull Corporation, with its outdated, largely medieval and 'corrupt' electoral practices. Elections were held for the first time for a new, reformed, Corporation and George Cookman was amongst the new wave of more radical councillors elected. Now he was very much in the mainstream of local politics and civic life. He was prominent amongst those who raised funds for Hull's now famous Wilberforce Monument, became a Justice of the Peace and played a major role in the town for the rest of his life, occupying the position of mayor for two years in a row, from 1837. He retained his strong links with the abolitionists and in 1837, for example, he attended an anti-slavery meeting in the Mechanics Institute, in his capacity of mayor. He moved a vote of thanks after an address by R.M. Beverley on the iniquities of the apprenticeship system for ostensibly freed slaves.

During the later 1830s and beyond, George championed a range of radical causes. In 1835 he supported the locally born radical politician Thomas Perronet Thompson's narrow parliamentary election victory in the town [6; 20 June 1835]. In 1836 he was amongst those locals involved in petitioning Parliament in a call for a total repeal of stamp duties on newspapers [6; 12 Feb 1836]. The Hull petition was in support of the radical Francis Place, who led the parliamentary repeal campaign. George was vehement in his support for Place's campaign, stating that he considered the tax *'unjust and impolitic...inasmuch as it has a direct tendency to perpetuate ignorance amongst the people, especially the poor and working classes in the community.'* In the event, the 1830s repeal campaign failed but such duties, which artificially raised the cost of newspapers, were finally repealed in 1855, a few months before George's death.

George was also prominent, as Peronnet Thompson had been, in his support for the repeal of the Corn Laws, and played key roles in supporting wider economic and social change. He was a prominent supporter of the building and early operation of the Hull to Selby Railway, opened in 1840, and took a close interest in housing conditions and public health issues during the subsequent decades [6; 6 Mar 1840].

Meanwhile, George's eldest son, George Grimston, was encouraged by both parents, when growing up, to read widely–especially history books–and he had started work in his father's business whilst still in his teens. He too was a strong supporter and admirer of Wilberforce and the anti-slavery campaign and later named one of his children William Wilberforce Cookman. In 1821, young George was sent by his father on a business trip to relations in North America and whilst there he witnessed slavery at first hand. This clearly had a profound effect on him and he apparently resolved to preach the gospel and play some part in the emancipation of slaves in the southern states of the USA [7; p.5].

Back in England he discussed his plans with both parents and came to an agreement with his father that he would stay working for the family firm until he was twenty-five, then take up the Methodist Ministry, but in America, not Britain. During the years before his move to the USA he became an accomplished lay preacher. In an age of great public orators he developed a reputation for speaking, soon being described as a *'prince amongst platform orators'* [8; p. 12]. He was filled with a passion for his mission and the anti-slavery cause; shortly before sailing he is said to have noted that *'my heart exults to reflect that in a few months I may be permitted to preach Christ crucified to the poor blacks of Maryland'* [8; p. 14].

George Grimston emigrated to Philadelphia in spring 1825 and the following year became a minister of the Methodist Episcopal Church, returning only briefly to England in 1827 to marry Mary Barton, from Doncaster [6; 10 April 1827].

The preaching skills that George Grimston had nurtured in Hull were used to considerable effect in his American ministry. He earned a deserved reputation as a riveting orator and attracted large crowds wherever he spoke. Soon his circuit covered a whole county and his audiences included white and black alike. Though he developed a wide network of white friends and admirers in the southern states, he was continually affected by the all too apparent presence of slavery, as the celebrated author and former slave Frederick Douglass later wrote in his book *My Bondage and Freedom*:

Fig 5.1
Frederick Douglass, Civil Rights Activist

We slaves loved Mr. Cookman. We believed him to be a good man. We thought him instrumental in getting Mr. Samuel Harrison, a very rich slaveholder, to emancipate his slaves; and by some means got the impression that he was laboring to effect the emancipation of all the slaves. When he was at our house, we were sure to be called in to prayers. When the others were there, we were sometimes called in and sometimes not. Mr. Cookman took more notice of us than either of the other ministers. He could not come among us without betraying his sympathy for us, and, stupid as we were, we had the sagacity to see it [4; p.63].

By 1838 George Grimston and his wife Mary, together with their five young children, moved to Washington, where he was stationed at Wesley Chapel, quite close to the Capitol. His reputation drew large crowds and his congregation included many members of Congress. Not long afterwards, he was elected Chaplain to the Senate. This was an old post by US constitutional standards, having been created when Senate had first convened in New York in 1789, and chaplains of all denominations had subsequently served in the role.

At this time the Cookmans, father and son, were at the zenith of their political careers and for a short time father and son occupied concurrently and respectively the offices of Mayor of Hull and Chaplain to the US Senate, where the latter's preaching was regularly reported in the press and continued to attract politicians of all political persuasions.

George senior had paid a visit to Philadelphia to see his son and young family in 1831 [6; 22 Nov 1831], but had not seen them since. When George Grimston's term of office ended in 1841 he determined to make a trip back home to visit his ageing father. By this time George, a widower since Mary's death in 1829, having no family left to take over the business, as his other son had died and his daughter had emigrated to South Africa, had sold his business and settled into Stepney Lodge (now the site of Beverley Road Baths and Stepney Primary School).

Tragedy struck. George Grimston bid his young family farewell and embarked on the steamship *President* in May 1841. Neither the ship nor those on board were ever seen again. No one knows for certain what happened to the vessel, although the common belief is that it foundered in violent storms which were raging for days off the North American coast.

Fig 5.2

The steamship 'President' which disappeared at sea in 1841.

Such a loss brought grief to Cookman family members on both sides of the Atlantic. George senior sought to persuade his distraught daughter-in-law to bring her young family back to England but Mary determined to remain, saying her husband would have wished it. The family moved to a small house in Baltimore, George senior provided support from the UK and his grandchildren were able to continue with their education. The eldest boys, Alfred and George, regularly corresponded by letter with their grandfather and thus they were provided with support and spiritual guidance from both sides of the Atlantic. They, too, were to follow in family footsteps and both eventually became Methodist ministers, with Alfred embarking on his preaching career from around the age of eighteen in Baltimore [7; p.14].

Over the following couple of decades Alfred was to become one of the most eminent and influential preachers in the USA. He inherited his father's skills as an orator and there was said to be no minister in the Baltimore Episcopal Church circuit who could draw a larger crowd. Throughout this time he remained in regular correspondence with his grandfather and in summer 1850 crossed the Atlantic in the steamer *Europe* to visit him at home in Stepney Lodge, Hull. They evidently got on well and he stayed for more than two months, making his mark amongst Hull's Wesleyan Methodist community when he preached at a number of local chapels, being particularly pleased, in his words, that he *'blew my trumpet in old George Yard where Wesley, Benson and my beloved father have been heard.'*

George senior died in 1856 and was buried in Withernsea Churchyard [2; p.17]. By this time, Alfred had married Annie Brunner, from Columbia, Pennsylvania, and over the following years he took up various ministries on the eastern coastal states of the USA. The family's skills as orators were said to have been inherited more from

Alfred's grandmother Mary than from George senior, who was by all accounts a more reserved speaker. What is clear, however, is that Alfred had inherited the Cookman family's long-standing and vehement opposition to slavery.

Fig 5.3
Sketch of Alfred Cookman

Alfred rose to the peak of his powers and influence at the very time that America's divisions over slavery were widening, and relations between the northern and southern states deteriorated. This growing rift was also evident amongst members of the Episcopal Methodist Church, and Alfred was prominent amongst those who wished to see the complete abolition of slavery. In May 1860 he attended the church's General Conference in Buffalo, where a motion to exclude those holding slaves was to be debated [7; pp.25-26]. The motion was passed, to the chagrin of a number of southern white members of the church but, as far as Alfred and his fellow anti-slavery supporters were concerned, the battle lines had been drawn.

The resultant schism in the Methodist Episcopal Church reflected the political fault lines of the United States, which became even wider after the election in 1861 of Abraham Lincoln, a known opponent of slavery, as President of the United States.

After the outbreak of the Civil War, Alfred moved to New York. The following summer, at an immense war gathering held in Lancaster, he made a passionately patriotic speech, praising the values of the union:

> This union, which is so unutterably dear to our hearts, is at the present time in imminent peril...a government closely connected with the cause of liberty throughout the world...must be preserved and perpetuated in all its purity and integrity. (Cheers) [8; pp.151-152].

In January 1863 President Lincoln issued his famous Emancipation Proclamation.

All slaves were declared to be free. Although the justice and expediency of this were questioned by some in the northern states at the time, the New York Episcopal Methodists soon showed their strong public support for the move, at a conference held in Washington Square Church. Here, Alfred was to the fore of Lincoln's champions and he prepared a war report, which was adopted with little opposition. This contained ten resolutions declaring unconditional support and loyalty to the USA and Unionist cause. The Fifth Resolution unequivocally declared:

> That slavery is an evil, incompatible in its spirit and practice with the principles of Christianity, with republican institutions, with the peace and prosperity of our country, and with the traditions, doctrines and discipline of our Church. [8; pp. 154-156].

Abraham Lincoln was later to say that no church did so much to support the Government in its efforts to maintain the Union as did the Methodist ministers.

In early 1864 Alfred visited the Army of the Potomac in its winter quarters on the front, preaching and, although not in good health, he covered a great deal of ground, spending four weeks riding over country made desolate by the actions of war. After the Civil War ended, Alfred remained in the vanguard, this time as a supporter of granting full rights of citizenship to freed slaves and of providing opportunities of elevation for all of them, through education:

> It must be left to Providence and to the colored people themselves. We cannot force them away; it would be unwise, unkind, unchristian and to colonize as we have been doing is like emptying a river by taking out a bucketful every now and then. Let us live for the present, faithfully discharging the duty of the passing hour which is to educate and elevate a people whose unrequited labor, multiplied wrongs, tedious bondage and deep degradations give them a special claim upon us. Give them the spelling book, the bible, equal rights before the law and the electoral franchise as their weapons of defence and then leave all the rest to God [8; p.186].

During the remainder of the 1860s Alfred Cookman was a prominent member of the Holiness Movement, a group of pastors who professed the experience of sanctification. He proved an avid supporter of Methodist summer camps and regularly preached at these gatherings. His family eventually moved to New Jersey, where he acquired a summer cottage on the edge of the ocean. By now his health was failing, although he continued to preach and to visit summer camps almost to the end. One of his last sermons was attended by President Ulysses Simpson Grant in October 1871. He died the following month at the age of forty-three and was interred in Laurel Hill Cemetery, Philadelphia, one of the most revered resting places in the USA.

The Cookman name did not die with Alfred. The summer cottage retreat eventually became part of Asbury Park, named after Francis Asbury, whom Wesley had sent to take the Wesleyan message to the USA. One of the main thoroughfares of the resort–now often associated with Bruce Springsteen–is called Cookman Avenue. Yet the most significant reminder of Alfred Cookman is in Florida. Before he died, Alfred is said to have given money towards the construction of the first building of the Cookman Institute [1]. Named after Alfred and opened in Jacksonville in 1872 by the Reverend Alfred Darnell, the Cookman Institute, affectionately known as *Old Cooky,* was the first institute of higher education for blacks in the state of Florida. In 1924 it was merged with the Daytona Normal and Industrial Institute of Daytona Beach, which had been founded for Negro girls in 1904 by Dr. Mary McLeod Bethune. It is now known as Bethune-Cookman University and today provides a distant but lasting reminder of nineteenth-century Methodism, liberty and Hull's anti-slavery movement[1].

Fig 5.4
The Cookman Institute, Jacksonville, Florida, founded 1872.

---

1   See also Robb Robinson, Far Horizons: from Hull to the Ends of the Earth (Hull, 2010) p. 127.

References

1. *African American Registry* http://www.aaregistry.org/historic_events/view/cookman-institute-right-place-and-time (accessed 2 December, 2013)

2. Cookman, E.M., *The Life of George Cookman 1774 – 1856*, (Hull, 1995 updated version March 1998, copy in Hull History Centre)

3. Cookman, George, *A Vindication of Principles and Good Character Occasioned by the Late Proceeding in the Methodist Society in the Town* (Hull, 1835) 20.

4. Douglass, Frederick, *Narrative of the Life of Frederick Douglass, an American Slave* (USA, 1845, re-published on-line Forgotten Books, 2008, www.forgottenbooks.org) 63.

5. *Hull Advertiser*

6. *Hull Packet*

7. McDonald, William, *Life Sketches of the Rev. Alfred Cookman* (USA: Freedmen's Aid and Southern Education Society, 1900), digitised version, http://wesley.nnu.edu/wesleyctr/books/0801-0900/HDM0859.PDF) 5.

8. Ridgeway, Henry B., *The Life of Alfred Cookman* (New York, 1875, digital edition by Holiness Data Ministry, 2/7/1998).

Mary Murdoch: Hull's 'Lady Doctor'

Marie Holmes

Hull and Human Rights–If you were asked to name someone who met both of those criteria, how would you answer? William Wilberforce's name would probably be the one that most people would give because of his well documented campaign to abolish the slave trade.

A less well-known individual with links to Hull who campaigned for human rights all her life is Dr Mary Murdoch. Although not born in Hull, she made a significant impact in the town as a doctor and a campaigner for the suffrage (for women to be granted the right to vote in national elections). Mary holds the distinction of being the first woman General Practitioner in Hull, a role in which she strove to improve living and health conditions for the people of the town. She also used her home and surgery on Beverley Road to hold meetings to organise the suffrage campaign and promote the involvement of women in activities and careers outside the traditional domestic sphere.

Mary Charlotte Murdoch was born in Elgin, Scotland, on 26 September 1864. She was the youngest of seven children born to Jane and William Murdoch. Her father, a solicitor, died when she was twelve, leaving her mother with the sole responsibility of raising and educating the children. Hope Malleson, in her biography of Mary, published three years after Mary's death, writes:

> She [Mrs Murdoch]...did not bring up her daughters to think of earning their livelihood or prepare themselves for any career save that of domesticity and marriage, and the life her youngest daughter chose would have evoked no sympathy from her had she lived to know of it [2; p.4].

Mary was first educated at home by a governess, then at a local school, and when she was fifteen she was sent to Manor Mount Girls' Collegiate School, at Forest Hill, London. She was described as a gifted scholar during her schooldays, and prepared to stand up for the rights of others - perhaps an early indication of a trait that would be apparent in her work in her adult life.

> At this period of her girlhood she was a great admirer of Carlyle and his gospel of work. She called herself a Liberal and a Home Ruler and had already cut herself adrift from the religious teaching of her childhood [2; p 10].

Fig 6.1
Mary Murdoch as a young girl

Her time at the girls' school ended when she became ill, probably from a gastric ailment, which would recur throughout her life but which did not, her headmistress recalled, prevent her from being *'as active in body as in mind'* [2; p.10]. She then attended a girls' school in Switzerland, learnt Italian, became *'a good French scholar',* and travelled around Italy. At nineteen, like a dutiful daughter of those times, she returned to Elgin to live at home. She would spend the next four years there, the latter two caring for her sick mother. Later she would refer to this time as *'wasted years'.*

Following her mother's death Mary used a small inheritance she had received to move to London and in 1888 she entered the London School of Medicine for Women. It seemed that the idea of studying medicine had arisen from an article she had read about the need for women doctors in India. However, opportunities for women to study medicine were restricted at this time. Indeed, for a woman, a career in medicine was often viewed as a 'novelty'.

Many arguments were put forward about why a woman should not be allowed to have a career in medicine: she did not have the right temperament; there was no call for women doctors. Behind these arguments lay many men's fear of competing with women. Many of these arguments and fears mirrored those put forward about why women should not have the right to vote. But many women like Mary worked to overcome society's restrictions and pave the way for future generations of women to pursue careers not only in medicine but other areas previously denied to women.

Despite another bout of illness, Mary was, by all accounts, an exceptional, enthusiastic and hard-working student. Besides her medical training, she also maintained her keen interest in new ideas by reading and attending lectures on a wide variety of subjects, including women's suffrage. Her biographer adds:

> Hard work did not put a check upon her questing spirit, that insatiable craving for new ideas and search for truth wherever it might be found. She made time to hear Mrs Besant and Bradlaugh at the Secular Society's Rooms, Dr Voysey[1] at the Theistic Church...The lectures and publications of the Society for Psychical Research and the many meetings about this time for Woman Suffrage, awakened a keen interest...In these ways, and in reading George Eliot, Renan, Carlyle, Emerson, and, later, Benjamin Kidd, among others she rested from her absorption in the medical work [2; p.25].

On completion of her studies she worked for a short period in London and in 1893 she applied for the post of house-surgeon in the Victoria Hospital for Sick Children, in Hull. She was appointed, and the two years she spent at this hospital, *'one of the very few in Great Britain which welcomed women on its staff...gave her a great insight into the diseases of children.'* She moved back to a job in London but resigned that post due to ill health and returned to work in Hull in 1896, *'...at the urgent wish of friends she had made there'* [2; p.27].

Fig 6.2   Fig 6.3
Victoria Hospital for Sick Children and Mary Murdoch's Beverley Road surgery today

---

1   Voysey was curate of an Anglican church in Hessle from 1851 to 1858. He moved to a curacy in London and was sacked because he denied the doctrine of eternal punishment. He moved to a curacy near Tadcaster, Yorkshire, and was then tried as a heretic in York for denying the doctrine of everlasting Hell. Deprived of his living, he returned to London and founded the Theistic Church. His son CFA Voysey, born in 1857 in Hessle, became a notable architect and designer.

Her surgery was initially on Spring Bank but she later moved to larger premises at 102 Beverley Road as so many patients came to be treated by her. She also had consulting rooms in Grimsby and was appointed Honorary Assistant Physician to the Victoria Hospital for Sick Children, later Honorary Senior Physician, having become an acknowledged expert in the diseases of children. Her interest in the welfare of children extended to their rights, at a time when there were still instances of child labour and other exploitation of children in the United Kingdom. In a lecture, she says:

> *A great moral awakening is going on amongst us about children and their rights, and now that we are awake we women in particular must be up and doing and see that the children of the twentieth century surpass in every way all the generations of the past that have gone before* [2; p.203].

She was a determined and practical woman, not afraid of a challenge, and she often worked long hours at her medical practice and for the hospital's outpatients service. *'The doctor, her car* [she was one of the first women in Hull to own and drive a car] *and her little dogs, became one of the most familiar sights in the streets of Hull and the most welcome'* [2; p.32].

Fig 6.4
Mary Murdoch at work in her study

But Mary was not only an outstanding and successful doctor; she was also interested in politics and in the women's suffrage campaign. This issue of the vote for women was of great importance to her. She writes: *'I can't keep out of it, God planted the seed in me when I was born and I have watered it freely. Both my voice and my purse are at the service of the movement'* [2; p.87]. Her active involvement was inspired by her close friend Dr Louisa Martindale, who championed the improvement of the status of women in every field.

In 1900 when Louisa qualified as a doctor Mary had offered her the post of an assistant in her medical practice. Louisa accepted, aware that to work with such an outstanding GP would provide valuable experience. When Louisa arrived to share Mary's work and live in her house they began a campaign for the vote for women. In her book *Rebel Girls: Their Fight for the Vote,* Jill Liddington writes: *'It became a shared crusade, and they set about rousing Hull'* [1; p.170].

They started a Women's Suffrage Society, holding all the committee meetings in Mary's house. In 1897 many suffrage societies in Britain had merged to form the National Union of Women's Suffrage Societies (NUWSS) with the aim of gaining the vote for women 'as it was and may be' given to men. This would limit women's franchise, as it then was, to those with the required property qualifications, but it was thought that this plan would gain more support initially and lead eventually to a wider franchise.

The members, called suffragists, wanted to achieve their aim by legal and peaceful means, constitutionally. They campaigned by holding public meetings, presenting petitions to Parliament, writing letters to politicians, lobbying sympathetic Members of Parliament to sponsor Private Members' Bills for granting women the right to vote, publishing newspapers and distributing free literature.

The Hull branch of the National Union of Women's Suffrage Societies (NUWSS) was established in 1904 with Mary as its founding president. The Hull branch *'was active and effective from the start: the branch held monthly discussion meetings which soon attracted 200 members, formed satellite branches in neighbouring towns like Beverley, and presented a petition from the women of Hull to the House of Commons'* [1; p.171].

After Louisa left Hull in 1906, Mary continued to campaign for the suffrage. She inspired ten local women to stand for election as Poor Law Guardians (these were ad hoc Boards administering workhouses established by the 1834 Poor Law) and another stood for election as a city councillor. Indeed, she considered herself a driving force in highlighting the campaign in Hull and that if she had not acted many would not have been aware there was a campaign. She declared: *'If you don't belong to a suffrage society join one tomorrow, because if you are not represented in the affairs of your country, your work is not of so much value'* [2; p.177].

Mary travelled to local towns to gather more support and was often a NUWSS branch delegate on trips to London. These activities entailed much public speaking. She wrote: *'I longed at one time to be a preacher, and that is why I speak sometimes when I think I have a message'* [2; p.89]. She would probably have been aware of a speech made by a delegate to a suffrage societies conference in 1896:

> And what chance, I ask you, have we of getting Women's Suffrage, or of
> having numbers of women at elections pressing MPs for the suffrage, when
> we have all that much country unconcerned about it—unconverted? And

how shall they hear without a preacher? [4; p.68].

And Mary preached messages, spreading the word about women's suffrage, as well as practical and inspirational ones on medical matters and the education and advancement of women, some of which were published in Appendix II of Malleson's biography.

These activities were fitted in around the demands of her medical practice as, often fortifying herself with *'two raw eggs quickly swallowed'*, she prepared for an afternoon or evening's meeting or campaign. She wrote: *'I never have time to copy out or rearrange my things; I just sit down and make a few notes of the form I want it to take, then think a little, then reel the thing straight off'* [2; p.90].

Meanwhile, in 1903, Emmeline Pankhurst, along with two of her daughters, Christabel and Sylvia, who were all members of the NUWSS, left the organisation and formed the Women's Social and Political Union (WSPU). They were dissatisfied with the failure of the NUWSS to persuade Parliament to grant the vote to women and with its campaign strategy. Like the NUWSS, they wanted voting rights that were equal to those of men, under the existing franchise laws. Again, this meant that only middle-class women who met the property qualification would be granted the vote; this was criticised by anti-suffrage campaigners as demanding 'Votes for Ladies', not Votes for Women. Although many of the women in both groups came from middle- and upper-class backgrounds, radicals in both groups actively sought the participation of working-class women, as exemplified by Annie Kenney (a mill worker) and Mary Gawthorpe (a teacher from a working-class background), who held positions of responsibility in the WSPU.

'Deeds not Words' was the WSPU slogan, and in 1905 what was considered the first militant act took place: at a Liberal Party meeting in Manchester, Christabel Pankhurst and Annie Kenney interrupted Winston Churchill and Sir Edward Grey to ask whether they supported women's right to vote. At that time it was the custom for speakers to be listened to politely and in silence, even if you did not agree with them. When the women were ejected violently from the hall they began to hold a protest meeting outside and were arrested for obstruction. Their subsequent imprisonment for not paying the fine imposed gained the WSPU much public support. As a result of the WSPU's militant actions, *The Daily Mail* coined the word 'suffragettes' to distinguish them from the suffragists; the WSPU members did not mind the derisive diminutive: pronouncing the word with a hard 'g' indicated that they meant women to *get* the vote.

It was not unusual for women to be supportive of more than one group in the campaigns to win the vote; in many branch societies there were members who belonged to both the NUWSS and the WSPU. However, there is an accepted view that the NUWSS were the more peaceful protesters–'suffragists'–and that the WSPU were more militant–'suffragettes'–and these terms have been used by historians to differentiate between the types of campaigning undertaken by the women.

During its first few years the WSPU continued with the tactics of heckling prominent politicians, holding their own meetings and sending deputations to see the Prime Minister. The suffragettes' actions attracted the attention of the public to the cause, and the membership of both groups, especially that of the NUWSS, grew. The suffragists acknowledged the achievements of the WSPU and '...although the NUWSS never sanctioned militancy, the suffragists and the suffragettes worked together relatively harmoniously during the first few years of the WSPU's existence' [4: p.96].

In 1907 the NUWSS employed new campaign tactics. During elections they had a non-party policy, supporting candidates, whatever their party affiliation, who advocated the vote for women[2]. They rented shops in the towns in order to display and sell their literature and give information. They covered walls with notices, organised processions, gave out leaflets and held meetings.

> Their speakers often attracted such large audiences that the candidates' meetings were almost deserted, and this was especially to be desired when an 'anti' [a candidate opposed to women's suffrage] was addressing his electors [2; p. 92].

The campaigns were highly visual, using novel ways to highlight the cause, for example, producing card games which used the names of prominent women in the suffrage movement or making dolls in their likeness. Choirs were also formed to sing suffrage songs.

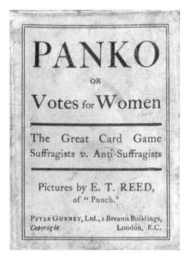

Fig 6.5   Fig 6.6

Suffrage doll and suffrage card game used to promote NUWSS campaigns

---

2   They also tried, unsuccessfully, to run a women's suffrage candidate, Bertrand Russell, in a by-election in Wimbledon in 1907.

Mary took part energetically and theatrically in these campaigns. In November 1907 when a by-election in the Hull West constituency was announced she wrote:

> To-morrow is the nomination day, when the candidates go to the Town Hall. I am going to drive through all the chief streets in a brake with a pair of chestnut horses to show them women mean to be in it [the election]. My seat on the box is very high, like a Highland coach, right over the horses. They are carrying the colours; my whip, with streamers of red, white, and green [suffrage colours[3]] advertising our big meeting...Even the dogs are wearing the colours [2; p. 93].

Liddington comments: *'Hull West took suffrage by-election choreography to new heights'* [4; p.174].

At a meeting around this time she *'had to reduce some fidgety youths at the back to order; they had come to scoff but remained to help, and signed the petition.'* Also, she was *'down in the hall afterwards with my hand on the shoulder of the dirtiest man in the room, trying to convince him that his wife had a mind!...a doctor's training is so wonderful that there is nothing in the world too dirty and too unclean for him to touch if he can help'* [2; p. 94].

During this by-election campaign Emmeline Pankhurst, a crowd-pulling speaker at by-election campaigns, visited Hull, as did her daughter Adela, to check that the party candidates would support the granting of the vote to women. In contrast to the NUWSS, the WSPU's policy was to oppose Liberal Party candidates because of their ruling party's failure to grant women the vote, and to oppose Labour Party candidates because the party had refused to include women's suffrage in its programme[4]. She was soon followed by Mary Gawthorpe, a member of the national committee, who arrived in Hull to try to form a branch of the WSPU.

At a packed public meeting, organised by the Hull branch of the NUWSS, to which the Labour and Liberal candidates in the by-election were invited and which Mary Murdoch chaired, the differences between the NUWSS and the WSPU in policy towards support for political parties and their different campaign tactics became apparent. Mary Gawthorpe, from her seat in the front row, began to heckle the Liberal candidate, whom she accused of not being fully committed, if elected, to support the franchise for women.

As the Liberal candidate *'picked up his hat "ready for escaping"'* when confronted by Gawthorpe's hostile questioning, and some suffragettes began to leave, Murdoch ruled that no more questions be asked of the candidate. She explained that the

---

3   The colours used in all forms of publicity were red, white and green for the NU-WSS, while purple, white and green were used by the WSPU in their campaigns.

4   Five years later, in 1912, the Labour Party declared its support for women's suffrage.

NUWSS was non-political, supporting both the Labour and Liberal candidates because both had promised to support the franchise for women. In the end, the Liberal candidate won the election and Gawthorpe's efforts to establish a branch of the WSPU were unsuccessful. Nonetheless, as Liddington notes: '...the Hull West contest showed that the suffrage campaign now reached almost right across the kingdom, out even to the fishermen on the North Sea docksides' [1; p.175].

However, as further Bills to enact women's suffrage were unsuccessful in Parliament, the WSPU's tactics became increasingly militant: civil disobedience, with the aim of provoking arrest; chaining themselves to railings; damaging government and business property; arson (setting fire to the mail in pillar boxes). In 1909 there were hunger strikes by suffragette prisoners in protest at the repeated imprisonment of many of their members and the denial of their demand for status as political prisoners. The public sympathised with them when the authorities began force feeding them so as not to be held responsible for any deaths.

In 1913 the country house of David Lloyd George, Chancellor of the Exchequer, was bombed, despite his support for enfranchising women Then there was the tragic incident at the Epsom Derby in 1913: Emily Wilding Davison, a WSPU campaigner, ran across the racecourse in an attempt, it is thought, to attach a suffragette banner to the King's horse, was trampled by it and died of her injuries. In 1914 a campaigner used an axe to slash a painting 'The Rokeby Venus', in the National Gallery, claiming that she was maiming a beautiful woman, just as the government was maiming Emmeline Pankhurst by force feeding her.

At first, the NUWSS admired the courage shown by the militant suffragettes and the publicity their actions brought to the campaign and did not criticise their tactics. However, as the violence escalated, in the hope of forcing Parliament to grant the vote to women, the NUWSS became concerned that these actions were harming the cause and in 1911 it announced publicly that it was dissociating itself from the increasingly militant tactics of the WSPU. Mary disagreed with this response and resigned from her position as president of the Hull branch. She considered it a matter of principle, but she did remain on good terms with the leader of the NUWSS.

In an address given in 1912 Mary explained her decision. She referred to the different campaign strategies but believed that, whatever the tactics or methods women employed, there should be loyalty amongst the groups of women working for a common cause (indeed, 'The Common Cause' was the title of a NUWSS journal). She believed that it was wrong to condemn publicly those who used militant tactics. She spoke about tolerance:

> Because our sisters' methods are not exactly the same as ours, do not let us rush wildly into print and proclaim on the housetops how wrong they are. For all we know, their methods may be very much better than ours...We are all fighting for the same great cause; let us each fight as well as we can, with brain and heart and mind. Public dissensions between women do more harm than any hard fighting. [2; p. 221].

She was herself uneasy about the methods the WSPU used. Indeed, at that by-election meeting in 1907, she had been on the receiving end of the direct actions the WSPU employed, when speakers were repeatedly interrupted by its representatives. Gawthorpe would later apologise to Mary for the interruptions. Two years later Mary wrote to a friend that she would not condemn publicly other campaigners for the vote '...*even if death comes. Surely the only proper official course is to grant the suffrage*' [2; p.96]. Mary joined the WSPU and contributed funds, but she did not approve of the autocratic way in which it was run by Emmeline Pankhurst or with its militant policies. She never re-joined the NUWSS.

Mary's joining the WSPU, however, may have been more than a question of loyalty to the common cause, and may lie in the difference in ideology between the WSPU and the NUWSS. In *The Women's Suffrage Movement in Britain, 1866-1928,* [4] Sophia van Wingerden explains that the NUWSS:

> *...drew strength from the anti-suffrage arguments that men and women were different and argued that precisely because of the differences, women should have the vote...Although the suffragists sought the far-reaching reform of equality, their logic and rhetoric did not challenge the division of humanity into separate spheres at its root. It would be possible to give women the vote without upsetting the notion that women were now, and would remain, wives and mothers, first and foremost* [4; pp.102-103].

(In other words, because of their difference and therefore their particular interests, women should be elected to Parliament to represent those interests and points of view.)

> *...The WSPU, on the other hand, tended to reject arguments based on difference. Differences between men and women had been overestimated, they claimed, and in any case, equality was now the goal...Articles in* Votes for Women *and* The Suffragette, *the two WSPU periodicals, attempted to... prove woman's ability to enter the public sphere on the same and equal terms with man*' [4; pp.102-103].

Mary would have been knowledgeable about these debates about women's role and she may have realised that her public life as a doctor, a suffragist, and her efforts to encourage and assist women to participate in work outside the domestic sphere epitomised the new role for women to which the WSPU was committed.

While she was campaigning for the enfranchisement of women Mary was also working to advance their participation in the world of work outside the home. Malleson notes that:

> *As a doctor, Mary Murdoch had many opportunities of seeing how the*

spirit of dependence and the shirking of responsibility lowered the nervous stamina of women, quite apart from the injustice of many of the laws under which they lived, and which affected the condition of children. She was a strong advocate for the training that citizenship would give, and always felt that the enfranchisement of women would ameliorate the conditions of women's labour and increase their sense of responsibility, so that there should be less frivolity, gossip, and slander [2; pp. 94-95].

Mary's concerns clearly echo those expressed by Mary Wollstonecraft a century earlier. In fact, in a speech about the women's movement, she mentions Mary Wollstonecraft Godwin as being among those from whom *'We, too, have caught hold of the helping hand of our dear dead, for whom we must never cease to be thankful... who showed us our sins with keen satire...'* [2; p. 217].

Her encouragement of women into the workplace began from the time she was appointed to the Victoria Hospital for Sick Children, when *'none but women house-physicians and house-surgeons were appointed'* and she unstintingly gave them her knowledge, experience and support. Another doctor noted how Mary helped young girls

to escape from the bondage of the usual lazy unsatisfying life of the ordinary well-to-do household. An irate husband writes: "Before Dr Murdoch came bothering round I had an obedient household—my wife and daughters obeyed me in every way; but now—one has gone to be nurse in the infirmary, etc., etc." [2; p. 38].

In 1905 a Hull branch of the National Union of Women Workers[5], was formed, with Mary as its president, and she later became the national vice-president, representing the organisation at many international conferences. Mary established many projects to educate and support women. She started a crèche for children of women employed in factories, and as a training centre for young girls who wished to become nursemaids or mothers themselves. She founded a School for Mothers, worked at getting women elected to local Councils and took part in a deputation to the government to ask for the appointment of women patrols and police.

In all her activities for the betterment of women's lives, she was mindful, like Wollstonecraft, of the importance of the new relationship that would have to be forged between men and women:

---

5   Founded in 1895, its objectives were: 'The encouragement of sympathy of thought and purpose among the women of Great Britain and Ireland; the promotion of their social, civil and religious welfare; the gathering and distributions of serviceable information; the federation of women's organisations and the formation of local councils and Union of Workers.

Occasionally Dr Murdoch went down to the docks, and, standing upon an overturned box or tub, spoke to an attentive audience of dock labourers. Sometimes she would urge them to hold their babies for two hours every Sunday. It was good for the babies, she said, and in her mind the while was the knowledge of the rest it would be to the tired mothers. Some of the men did her bidding, and took an opportunity afterwards of telling her they had done so. [2; p.p. 108-109].

At the annual conference of the NUWW in 1913, held in Hull, she told the Congress:

Mothers should not be left to do all the drudgery while fathers take their ease...side by side with our schools for mothers we ought to have schools for fathers, so that both may take their share in this extremely difficult problem–the manufacture of our successors, the coming race. [2; p.126].

Her work as a doctor had of necessity brought Mary into contact with the poor and the conditions in which they lived. She wrote and spoke with personal knowledge and with great sympathy about the urgent need for improvements. In 1910 she had written:

We don't look after the houses of the poor yet enough...Now that we have gone to the poor and taken them as our sisters and brothers, I am hoping much may be done. We must go as their equals, and not as their superiors. How they do open their hearts to you when you sit on a corner of their kitchen-tables, and swing your leg there! and when most of your work amongst them is done with your sleeves turned up over your elbows, you seem just a working woman like themselves. [2; p. 97].

In a speech at the NUWW conference in 1911 in Glasgow, Mary expanded on this issue of insanitary living conditions and their effect on health, using statistics from an official pamphlet 'How the People of Hull are Housed', published by the Fabian Society in 1910. She was also speaking from her experience of working in Hull. However, this brought her into direct conflict with the Corporation of Hull and property owners, who were angry at the negative image they believed she had given of the town and accused her of misrepresenting the facts.

Despite attacks by officials, the local press and private and anonymous persons, Mary remained resolute and reiterated the points she had made. In speeches she gave in Hull and through written responses printed in the local newspapers, she explained her position and insisted that the facts she had quoted had come from an official source, from her personal experience of dealing with residents in the town and could also be found in the town's own official documents.

> *I have been all through the Census and Health Reports of the City for ten years, and verified all the Fabian figures. I little thought my Glasgow speech was going to create such a terrible local bother. I have all the facts and figures, and I am going to repeat my Glasgow paper, and give chapter and verse for all my statistics...* [2; p. 101].

Her statements were endorsed by the compilers of the Fabian pamphlet, and the public were made aware of the seriousness of poor housing conditions. Mary continued to attend national and international conferences, speak out and work for these causes even in the last years of her life when she suffered from recurrent ill health.

During these years Mary returned to organised religion, joining the Anglican faith in 1914. Her biographer comments that:

> *As to the religious sanctions for conduct, no one needed them less, for, through whatever phases she passed, she was an idealist...and the instinctive spurning of the ignoble, the mean, or self-seeking, and the obligation towards others and towards her life's work, were the outgrowth of her own character.* [2; p. 128].

She died on 20 March 1916, leaving an estate of £2,117 18s 11d (around £90,000 today). The many tributes written at the time of her death indicate that she made a significant impact on those around her. An obituary in The Lancet concludes:

> *She was an influential personality, she did much valuable public work when physically not equal to the strain, she was a woman of large sympathies, and invariably acted up to the high ideals and there is no doubt that in her the medical profession and women workers have lost an outstanding force for good.*

Her biographer records that:

> *Thousands gathered in the streets to testify their sorrow and love as her body was carried to the church from the consulting room in her house, whence no one in need had ever been turned away and friends coming from a distance realised, perhaps for the first time, that she had won the heart of an entire city.* [2; p.1].

Mary's rousing words from a speech she made about women's suffrage may serve as her epitaph:

Standing on an almost limitless shore, we can see, coming slowly in, the great rolling waves which go to make the inevitable high tide of women's progress, kept back often by seemingly impossible rocks and creeks, but still coming on. And no one can keep it back. [2; p. 88].

References

1. Liddington, Jill, *Rebel Girls fight for the Vote,* Virago, 2006
2. Malleson, Hope, *A Woman Doctor, Mary Murdoch of Hull,* Sidgwick & Jackson, 1919
3. Smith, Harold *British Women's Suffrage Campaign 1866-1928,* Longman, 1996
4. van Wingerden, Sophia, *The Women's Suffrage Movement in Britain, 1866-1928, Macmillan, 1999.*

Winifred Holtby: action for world peace, women's rights and racial harmony

Marion Shaw

Winifred Holtby was born on 23 June 1898, in Rudston, near Bridlington. She was the younger daughter of David Holtby and his wife Alice Holtby, neé Winn. David owned a prosperous farm at Rudston and came from a family who farmed successfully across an area that stretched from upstream Humber to Bridlington. Alice also came from a farming family; her father rented a mill and farm near Wensleydale. She was a large, vigorous, golf-playing, outspoken and opinionated woman, with youthful energy and enthusiasms even into old age. From quite a humble background she became a woman of importance when, four years after the family had given up farming and moved to Cottingham, she was elected in 1923 to East Riding County Council and in 1934 became the first woman to serve as an alderman. She was an ambitious and powerful mother who encouraged Winifred's writing talents and supported her university career (1917-1921) at Somerville College, Oxford, reading Modern History.

Fig 7.1
Rudston House: Winifred's birthplace

Winifred was first educated by a governess and then at Queen Margaret's School, a girls' boarding school in Scarborough. Her university career at Somerville College was interrupted by a year's service in 1918 as a member of the Women's Army Auxiliary Corps (WAAC) during the First World War. When she returned to Somerville College she met Vera Brittain, also returned from the war, where she had nursed in the Voluntary Aid Detachment (VAD). Vera became famous for *Testament of Youth* (1933), her account of her VAD experiences and the deaths of her fiancé, her brother and two close friends, soldiers killed during the war. As a result of these major losses she became a lifelong pacifist. Winifred and Vera became friends, a friendship that lasted throughout Winifred's life.

Winifred's generation of women received the vote on partial terms of equality with men in 1918. This, and the fact that so many of her male peers had been killed in the war, gave her and other women like her a sense of responsibility towards society. They considered themselves as women citizens. Winifred took her responsibilities seriously, becoming involved with Vera in pacifist and feminist activities. After they graduated, she and Vera moved to live together in London to lecture on these causes and to pursue their ideals of becoming writers. As well as journalism they both wrote novels. Winifred is chiefly remembered today for her novel *South Riding* (1936), set in the triangular area from Hull to Spurn Point and up the coast to Bridlington. It has never been out of print since its first publication and has been dramatised twice on television and once in film. She wrote five other novels, a large number of short stories, two volumes of poems, several non-fiction works and numerous articles for a range of journals from the *Radio Times* to the *Manchester Guardian.*

Fig 7.2
Winifred Holtby, probably in the garden of Holtby House, Cottingham

When they graduated from Somerville College both Vera and Winifred joined the League of Nations Union (LNU). This was one of many societies anxious to support *'some sort of international authority,'* as Leonard Woolf described it, *'in order to settle international disputes...and so help to keep the peace.'*[1] The international authority was the League of Nations (note the difference in name), which came into being in 1919 at the Paris Peace Conference, with a covenant of principles including collective security, arbitration of international disputes, reduction of armaments and open diplomacy. The idea of its founders was that the 'old diplomacy' of secret treaties and power struggles that seemed to have led to the First World War should give way to open diplomacy in which agreements would be accountable to democratic societies. The League of Nations was a focus of hope in the early 1920s but the exclusion of Germany from membership and the unwillingness of America to ratify its covenant meant that it was flawed from the beginning. The League of Nations Union was therefore a promotional organisation contributing to the League of Nations and working on its behalf. It was one of the largest and most active voluntary associations, with millions of Britons joining it, until its demise in the late 1930s. It relied on subscriptions and donations, and, for the most part, used unpaid speakers.

Winifred was one of these enthusiastic speakers, believing that *'a co-operative institution like the League of Nations, although imperfect, is better than armed neutralities or balances of power.'* Speakers like Winifred thoroughly endorsed the principle of democratic accountability but in order for this to be effective, ordinary citizens needed to be educated in what this might mean, particularly in the idea of international co-operation. As a historian she believed that the development of the nation state, with its extension into imperialism, had been necessary for civilisation but was now becoming obsolete and dangerous. *'The day of imperialism is passed,'* she wrote.

> *'[It] is really nothing more than dynamic and aggressive nationality... What we want now is the transition to a still wider sphere of international co-operation, where empires don't matter and patriotism becomes parochial, and the service of mankind becomes the only consideration.'*[2]

Winifred's idealism, fuelled by a sense of citizen responsibility now that women were becoming enfranchised, led her, often up to four times a week, to undertake *'long hot journeys in trains or long cold journeys in trams'* to make speeches or lead discussions on the League *'in almost every London suburb and in numerous small towns and villages all over the South of England and the Midlands.'* The work was often disheartening; at outdoor meetings she was frequently moved on by

---

1   Leonard Woolf, *Beginning Again: An Autobiography of the Years 1911-1918*, Harcourt Brace Jovanovich, 1963.
2   Winifred Holtby, *Letters to a Friend*, Collins, 1937. This heartfelt but vague message typified LNU thinking and was, as Susan Pederson has shown, 'strangely apolitical.' Co-operation was the watchword and matters of political disagreement and difficulty, such as the General Strike of 1926, were avoided.

the police, she was heckled, and she sometimes had to raise her own crowd. She learned how intransigent public opinion could be and how bigoted. Speaking to a group of intolerant and intolerable women–'wives of judges or diplomats'–she found their xenophobia, anti-semitism and imperialism 'a pitiable example of the mentality of erstwhile ruling classes,' in contrast to the schoolchildren, town councillors, trade unionists and the unemployed she had addressed the day before.

Alongside this, Winifred was also writing and lecturing on feminist issues, even though, as she said herself, she was a reluctant feminist, impatient that the battle for equal rights still needed to be won.

> I dislike everything that feminism implies...I want to be about the work in which my real interests lie, the study of inter-race relationships, the writing of novels and so forth. But while the inequality exists, while injustice is done and opportunity denied to the great majority of women, I shall have to be a feminist.

Her commitment to feminism took its most notable form in her membership of the Six Point Group and her involvement, eventually as a director, with the Group's journal, Time and Tide. The leading force behind both of these ventures was (Viscountess) Margaret Rhondda, a wealthy businesswoman who became one of Winifred's closest friends. Both women were equal rights feminists, believing in equality before the law and social betterment, through debate, petitions, meetings and lobbying to hasten the desired end of constitutional change. The Group's name derived from the six points of change it championed: satisfactory legislation on child assault, widowed mothers, unmarried mothers, the guardianship of children, and equal pay for men and women teachers, and equal pay for male and female civil servants. When one campaign was gained another point took its place.

In her early lectures Winifred made tentative attempts to link feminism and anti-militarism. 'Women do not make war...They know too well the value of human life, the cost at which it is brought into the world... But it is not enough for women to refrain from making war; they must make peace.'[3] When the rise of fascism in the 1930s threatened women's emancipation, Winifred wrote some of her most impassioned journalism on this topic. In an article of 1934, 'Shall I Order a Black Blouse?' she wrote that 'At present I feel and think as an individual; if the Blackshirts were victorious, I should be expected to think only as a woman.' The Blackshirt motto that 'We want men who are men and women who are women' represented to Winifred a creed 'which wherever practised has resulted in an attempt at sex segregation.'

She also wrote a play, Take Back Your Freedom. Never performed in Winifred's life-time, this brought together her pacifism and her feminism in a leading character based on Oswald Mosley, the fascist 'black shirts' leader, whose heightened masculinity is the counterpart of his adoring mother's frustration at the constraining feminine role

---

3   Winifred Holtby, South African Lady's Pictorial, 1926.

she has been forced into because participation in public life has been denied her as a woman. The implied message of the play is that masculinity and femininity are social constructs exaggerating differences between men and women that lead to aggression in men and passivity in women.

Fig 7.3
With George Bernard Shaw and Margaret Rhondda at the Malvern Festival, July 1935

Winifred's writing on all subjects was dominated by an overarching ideal, what she called 'a human ideal' in which people are seen as individuals, and not categorised according to race, religion or gender: *'Neither Jew nor Gentile, male nor female, bond or free.'* As she wrote to her mother towards the end of her life, her aim throughout had been to see an end to inequalities of all kind, to persuade people to *'recognise the human claims of Negroes and Jews and women and all oppressed and humiliated creatures.'* This commitment involved her in the cause that in some respects was the most important of her life. It had its origins in her interest since childhood in South Africa. When Vera Brittain married in 1926 it seemed to Winifred that this was an opportunity for her to fulfil a lifelong dream of visiting that country.

She went to lecture for the LNU and to see Jean McWilliam, the friend she had met when working in France during the war. Jean had moved to South Africa and become the headmistress of a girls' school in Pretoria. Winifred also met the novelist Ethelreda Lewis, who recognised in her a passion for social justice which could be useful in promoting better working conditions for black workers. White liberals in South Africa like Mrs Lewis were fearful on two related counts: that unless these conditions improved there would be violent racial conflict and that during this the black population would turn to Communism. These two dangers, she believed, could be averted by the growth of a black trade union movement based on a British model. This was where Winifred might be helpful.

The mid-1920s were crucial years for South African race relations. Black unrest was increasing as a result of recent legislation consolidating the supremacy of white labour, and the intensification of segregationist policies which were driving black workers further into poverty and degradation. The Industrial Consolidation Act of 1924 had rendered the term 'employee' inapplicable to black workers and thereby barred them from, among other benefits, trade union membership. The Mines and Works Acts of 1926 specifically excluded Africans and Coloureds from obtaining certificates of competency; this exclusion meant that they were restricted to low-paid, unskilled work. It was generally acknowledged that white wages (the highest in the world) could only be paid for by the sweated labour of black workers. This was a situation which the South African Trade Union movement and the Labour Party supported.

Mrs Lewis's focus was on an existing 'informal' union, formed in 1919 from an amalgamation of two groups involved the year before in a dock strike, which she thought had great potential as a force for change. This was the black Industrial and Commercial Workers' Union (ICU), and its leader was Clements Kadalie. The son of a Nyasaland[4] chief, he was a man of great charm, energy and recruiting ability, and an impassioned speaker. He was, as Winifred would later describe him, 'suspicious, sensitive, vain' and also easily influenced. Under Kadalie's leadership, the ICU during its first five years was astonishingly successful. More than a trade union in the British sense, it was a social, political, religious and educational force which served to unite black people from different kinds of employment and different areas, both rural and urban. Its membership was 80,000 by 1927 and its annual income £12,000.

Fig 7.4
Clements Kadalie, leader of the ICU, South Africa

---

4 Nyasaland is now Malawi.

But as its size increased its weaknesses became apparent: poor financial and administrative management, a hostile political context, divided loyalties amongst its officials, inexperience in trade union organisation and lack of support from fraternal organisations which did not acknowledge its existence. It was to address some of these weaknesses that Mrs Lewis and other white liberals were keen to act, and Winifred seemed an appropriate person to supply at least some of these needs by gaining support from the British trade union movement.

Winifred described herself as a *'passionate imperialist by instinct.'* The paternalistic organisation of her father's farm provided a model of how such a society could function. As Leonard Woolf pointed out, to liberals during the inter-war years, 'imperialism' was not the dirty word it later became. He, like Winifred, believed in Britain's parental responsibility towards the territories she had acquired, which would include a programme of gradual and educative devolution of power towards equal citizenship and self-government. The transfer of power should involve the granting of dominion status to those capable of sustaining it, and a mandate system on a trustee principle for countries insufficiently developed to be self-regulating. In each case, the franchise should be extended on a cultural rather than a racial basis. In 1926 Winifred could not have foreseen how this idealistic, and probably naive, programme of reform would encounter such intractable difficulties and obstacles. By the time of her death in 1935 she had begun to realise the complexities of this troubled nation, and her novel *Mandoa, Mandoa!,* set in a mythical African country, acknowledges this.

On her return home from South Africa Winifred's first task in the cause of black trade unionism was to alert the British Independent Labour Party (ILP)[5] to the situation and also the British trade union movement. She inserted an appeal in the *New Leader*, the ILP's newspaper, on behalf of the ICU libraries in Durban and Johannesburg. She pointed out that many black workers had moved into the cities and had lost touch with their cultural roots. The ICU was aiming to educate them in new ideas and ways of life for which up-to-date books were needed. The response was good and Kadalie acknowledged receipts of parcels of books in a letter which also asked Winifred to make contact with British politicians and labour leaders.

After canvassing a number of individuals Winifred finally made contact with Arthur Creech Jones, General Secretary of the Transport and General Workers Union and a member of the ILP Industrial Advisory Committee. Kadalie himself wrote to Creech Jones urging action; it was time, Kadalie said, that *'the British Labour Movement should interest itself in the position of South African Native workers.'* Creech Jones advised Kadalie to be cautious in his management of the ICU, not to inflame racial hatred, or engage in politics to disparage the white Government or be sidetracked by Communism, but concentrate on *'the capacity of the Union to cater for the industrial needs of the natives.'* Kadalie seems to have taken this advice seriously in that he created a 'constitution' which Winifred appears to have been involved in drafting. This stated, amongst much else, that the union *'shall not foster or encourage antagonism*

---

5   The ILP was a socialist organisation, established in Bradford in 1893 as a political party. From 1906 to 1932 it was affiliated to the Labour Party.

towards other established bodies, political or otherwise, of African peoples, or of organised workers.'[6]

In spite of this apparently moderate document, Kadalie was proving worrying to the white supporters in South Africa in his use of wild language at conferences and his reluctance to sever connections with the Communists. It was a relief to Mrs Lewis that he decided to visit England to advance the cause of the ICU, arriving at Southampton in May 1927. He noted with delight that the dockers at Southampton were white, that a white porter carried his luggage, that the train to London was not segregated and most of all that a 'tall young Englishwoman' (Winifred) had greeted him in London, shaken hands and driven off with him in a taxi, much to the surprise of the white South Africans who had shunned him on the boat.

Winifred, Creech Jones and Fenner Brockway (secretary) had managed to interest the ILP to some small degree in Kadalie's visit and had arranged a lecture tour for him throughout England and Scotland so that he could publicise the ICU. The tour was flattering and encouraging but little in the way of tangible support was forthcoming, including financial support. There was a general fear that support for the ICU could antagonise other sections of the trade union movement, including the South African trade unions.

Kadalie's visit to London increased Winifred's commitment to him and to the union and also her belief that the development of a black trade union was the way forward so that eventually association with white trade unionism would be possible. *'I am sure,'* she wrote, *'that Kadalie is going on the right lines when he works for this. The gulf between black and white labour must ultimately be fatal for South Africa.'* What seemed to her to be the ICU's most urgent need was effective organisation and the idea took root that an experienced trade union organiser from Britain should visit South Africa to help the ICU on its administrative side. Winifred and Creech Jones were given the task of finding a suitable candidate and after some months of canvassing she was approached by William George Ballinger from Motherwell, an idealistic and hardworking local government activist, but with little trade union experience. In any event, by the time he reached South Africa in June 1928 the situation with the ICU was almost beyond the remedial capabilities of any official.

The ICU was rapidly descending into chaos, with branches disaffiliating, the treasury empty, unscrupulous lawyers, and personal feuds and rival organisations springing up everywhere. Where other men would have hastened home, Ballinger persevered, eventually working to promote co-operative ventures in farming, catering and retail. His salary was rarely paid by the ICU during the years he worked for it, a deficit which Winifred personally filled with help from friends and fund-raising activities and publicity, including her impassioned journalism on issues such as segregation, racist legislation and the plight of black people in Britain. *'I must have written literally millions of words about Ballinger since 1927,'* she wrote to Vera in 1934.

---

6   Quoted Marion Shaw, The Clear Stream: A Biography of Winifred Holtby, Virago, 2000.

Fig 7.5

The Winifred Holtby Memorial Library, built in 1940 in a Johannesburg township, South Africa (moved to Soweto in 1963 and destroyed in the 1976 riots).

Kadalie resigned in disgrace in 1929, a tragic lost opportunity to harness and direct the power of the ICU in its early stages. It is easy to accuse Winifred of naivety in her involvement in South African affairs. She seriously underestimated the importance of racial issues to the development of trade unionism, believing, as she frequently stated, that there were similarities between black workers and working-class labour in Britain. Kadalie may have been distracted from his leadership of the ICU by European (and white South African liberal) interference, but the task was almost certainly too great for him, perhaps for any individual at that time. Winifred never gave up hope in the ICU cause, at least not in her public pronouncements, except, perhaps, in her novels. In *Mandoa, Mandoa!* the main female character, a projection of Winifred herself, facing intractable problems, expresses her dogged refusal to accept failure: *'we have to work for the world as we know it as best we can... we have to go on.'*

By the time *Mandoa, Mandoa!* was published Winifred was seriously ill. Severe headaches and nausea were first attributed to overwork but in 1932 renal sclerosis (Bright's disease) was diagnosed. She was told that she probably had only two years to live, information she kept from others until her condition worsened to such an extent that friends and relatives had to be told. She filled her remaining years with an astonishing amount of work and service to others, not least, as far as her reputation is concerned, the writing of *South Riding*. She died on 29 September 1935 in

83

a London nursing home. After a London memorial service at St Martin-in-the-Fields she was taken for burial in All Saints Churchyard, Rudston. Her gravestone gives the dates of her life, that she was the daughter of David and Alice Holtby and the inscription *'God give me work till my life shall end And life till my work is done.'* Although the inscription is appropriate, it insufficiently informs those who visit the grave of her great achievements as a social reformer and writer.

Fig 7.6
Winifred's grave, in the churchyard of All Saints Church, Rudston

Further Reading

1. Vera Brittain, *Testament of Friendship,* Virago [1940], 1980

2. Winifred Holtby, *Letters to a Friend,* edited by Alice Holtby and Jean McWilliam, Collins, 1937

3. Winifred Holtby, *Mandoa, Mandoa!* Virago [1933], 1980

4. Susan Pederson, 'Triumph of the Poshocracy,' *London Review of Books,* 8 Aug. 2013, pp. 18-20.

5. Marion Shaw, *The Clear Stream: A Biography of Winifred Holtby*, Virago, 2000

Lillian Bilocca and Hull's fighting fishwives

Hands that rocked the cradle...and actions that shook the world

Brian W Lavery

Mrs Lillian Bilocca, also known as *Big Lil* (1929-1988), was the leader of a high-profile campaign by Hull trawlermen's wives to improve working and safety conditions for that industry in the late 1960s. She was born in a 'two-up, two-down' at Villa Terrace, Wassand Street, Hull, East Yorkshire, in the city's Hessle Road fishing community, on 26 May 1929, as the eldest of four daughters of Ernest and Harriet Marshall. Ernest had been a Royal Navy engineer and then later a trawlerman. Harriet was a housewife.

Lillian's education at Daltry Street Junior School ended at the age of just fourteen and she joined a local fish house as a cod skinner. Like her peers, she went from being a seafarer's daughter to a seafarer's wife and later a seafarer's mother.

She had two children, Ernest (b. 1946) and Virginia (b. 1950), with Carmelo 'Charlie' Bilocca, (b.1902) who was a Maltese merchant sailor with the Hull-based *Ellerman-Wilson Line*. He settled in the city and later worked as a trawlerman. Lillian, Charlie and the children lived in Coltman Street, Hull, off Hessle Road.

After Charlie's death in 1981 at the age of seventy-nine, Lillian moved to the nearby Thornton Estate, where she ended her days, a stone's throw from her birthplace; and that would have been her life–told in the *hatch, match and dispatch* columns of the local paper, like others of her class and time–had it not been for remarkable events in 1968.

Fig 8.1
Civic plaque on the flats on the site of the old Victoria Hall

Fig 8.2
Portrait photo of Mrs Bilocca

(both pictures courtesy of Dr Alec Gill MBE)

85

Aged thirty-nine, Lillian became a household name as the impromptu leader of a 'fishwives' army' fighting for better safety at sea following the Hull Triple Trawler Disaster during the 'Dark Winter' of 1968. The *St Romanus, Kingston Peridot* and *Ross Cleveland* sank with the loss of fifty-eight men between January 11 and February 4, in ferocious Arctic waters. This was the biggest peacetime UK fishing disaster of the 20th century.

Lillian and the Hessle Road Women's Committee went from lobbying trawler bosses to being invited to Westminster and fighting their case in the glare of the world's media, forcing huge changes in trawler safety in an incredibly short time, saving countless future lives.

The *St Romanus* sank with all hands on January 11, 1968, as did the *Kingston Peridot* on January 26, and on February 4 only one man (the mate Harry Eddom) survived the sinking of the *Ross Cleveland*.

Fig 8.3
Front cover of the 40th anniversary souvenir paper for the Triple Trawler Disaster, showing the three doomed ships. (Reproduced by kind permission of the Hull Daily Mail).

Into the late 1960s, trawlermen worked in the most dangerous industry on Earth. The Standard Mortality Rate (SMR) for UK fishermen was seventeen times that of other workers and more than five times that of the next most dangerous job—coal mining. [4; p. 11]. These harsh conditions contributed to catastrophic loss of lives in early 1968.

86

The *St Romanus* had no radio operator. There were no lifelines or adequate safety rails. Moreover, any protective or safety clothing was to be bought by the men. Crews provided their own bedding, bought from a 'company store'.

Trawl fishing was still governed by the final 'master and servant' Act in force in the 20th century–The Merchant Shipping Act of 1894. A man could be jailed for not showing up for work.

The 1968 disaster led to the trawlermen's wives of Hessle Road taking direct action. After the *St Romanus* and the *Kingston Peridot* had been declared lost and before the fate of the *Ross Cleveland* was known, Lillian and others gathered thousands of signatures demanding better safety. She and her fellow 'fishwives' organised a meeting at a local community hall on Friday, February 2, 1968.

An estimated 600 women attended, and among those speaking was local National Union of Seamen firebrand John Prescott. He went on to become the Member of Parliament for East Hull from 1970 and Deputy Prime Minister from 1997-2010. He was made a Labour peer in 2011.

Local Labour MP James Johnson was also at the meeting, along with Transport and General Workers' Union (TGWU) officials as well as left-wing activists from Hull University. But these angry working-class women were in no mood for politicians and union men and middle-class Marxist lecturers.

Lillian, in her fish worker's headscarf and apron, addressed the women: *'Right lasses, we're here to talk about what we are going to do after the losses of these trawlers. I don't want any of you effin' and blindin'. The press and TV are here.'*
In the highly charged atmosphere the women marched on the owners' offices, but the 'headscarf army' were fobbed off. Lillian told the crowd: *'There is only one way to make these people meet us and hear our case and that's by taking action.'*

Just a little more than ten hours later, in the early morning of Saturday, February 3, she and a small group of women tried to stop the *St Keverne* leaving dock. Under the erroneous impression that no radio controller was on the trawler, Lillian attempted to board it. Photographs of the seventeen-stone housewife struggling with police, who prevented her boarding, hit the headlines. A Sunday tabloid dubbed her 'Big Lil' and a media star was born. She was to be lionised and patronised in equal measure by the Press, a cross between Boudicca and Nora Batty.

Some women were angered by Lillian's action. Superstitions were strong, and many felt that a woman on the dock was bad luck and would 'wave the men away' to their doom. Superstition was embedded in this community and even in comparatively modern times it was enough to prevent almost half of 600 or so joining in the dockside march after the meeting. Perhaps the constant proximity to death and the expectation of tragedy caused this to be so [2; p. 15].

Fig 8.4
'Marching on the bosses': Taken after the Victoria Hall meeting and shows Mrs. Bilocca leading a march on the owners' offices. (Reproduced by kind permission of the Hull Daily Mail)

This reaction may seem odd when viewed from outside this close community, but the feeling was strong enough to be partly used against Lillian later to drop her from the Women's Committee.

The tide turned quickly in the women's favour when a third ship sank. On Sunday, February 4, 1968, Skipper Philip Gay of the ill-fated *Ross Cleveland* transmitted this final, desperate message to his friend Skipper Len Whur of the *Kingston Andalusite*, who watched helplessly as the Cleveland sank: *'I am going over. We are laying over. Help us, Len, she's going. Give my love and the crew's love to the wives and families.'* Skipper Whur saw the *Ross Cleveland* sink during a blizzard and hurricane in an Icelandic fjord, but was powerless to help.

Lillian's son Ernie Bilocca, aged twenty-one, was a deckhand under Skipper Whur.

Trawler owners, who had recently snubbed the women, now asked to see them to discuss their demands. The women drew up a *Fishermen's Charter* demanding:

Full crews, including radio operators for all ships
Twelve-hourly contacts between ships and owners while trawlers were at sea
Improved safety equipment from the owners
A 'mother ship' with medical facilities for all fleets
Better training for crews and a safety representative on each ship
Suspension of fishing in winter on the northern Icelandic coast that claimed the three trawlers and
A Royal Commission into the industry.

When news of the sinking of the *Ross Cleveland*–apparently lost with all hands—

reached Hull, Lillian and two others waited to meet with the owners and saw one of their colleagues, co-organiser Christine Smallbones, being comforted by a clergyman. He confirmed to her that the *Ross Cleveland,* skippered by her brother Philip Gay, was lost.

A photograph of this moment was on the front of the *Daily Mirror* the next day.

Fig 8.5

Daily Mirror, front page from February 6, 1968, provided by ukpressonline.co.uk

The women took their case to Westminster. Grief-stricken Christine stayed in Hull. The local TGWU arranged the meeting, and the women met with Minister of Agriculture Fred Peart and the Minister of State at the Board of Trade J. P. W. Mallalieu.

Not since the Russian Navy's sinking of the Hull fishing fleet in 1904, when commanders of that country's Imperial Navy mistook trawlers for Japanese torpedo boats, had such shockwaves run through that community as when the news of the *Ross Cleveland's* fate became known.

Lillian Bilocca, Yvonne Blenkinsop and Mary Denness set off for London with ten thousand signatures, their *Fishermen's Charter* and a media circus in tow. Lillian had earlier told the Press she would march on Downing Street or even *'that Harold Wilson's private house,'* if she was not heard. Peart and Mallalieu were told by Prime Minister Harold Wilson that the women were to be helped as much as possible.

As they set off for London, the *Hull Daily Mail* reported:

The wives, led by 39-year-old Lillian Bilocca, were laughed off at first by many in the fishing industry. But now it is accepted that they mean business. What could have turned out to be a hysterical, disorganised protest is now becoming regarded as something of a fighting machine, backed by hundreds.

Mrs Mary Denness recalled how, at King's Cross, the platforms were empty and that she, Lillian and Yvonne were the only 'real' passengers on the train: *'It was full of journalists, union men, photographers and TV folk. When we got off, the station was empty and the platforms were surrounded by those barriers they use on royal visits.'* But when they got to the exit there were thousands waiting and cheering. A newspaper billboard read: 'BIG LIL HITS TOWN.'

The women had a meeting with the ministers, after which they learned that the mate of the *Ross Cleveland*, Harry Eddom, had been found alive. The story of his survival and how the two crewmates he shared a lifeboat with, bosun Walter Hewitt and galley boy John Barry Rogers, had perished became worldwide news.

The eyes of the world were on the Hull fishing community–and the politicians and owners knew it.

The women were delighted at the news of Eddom's survival and the immediate promises from the MPs. Upon their return, Lillian later told the Press at Hull Paragon Station it was the *'happiest day of her life.'*
'We've done it!' she said.

The action taken was very swift. Fishing off the Northern Cape of Iceland was suspended immediately until the weather improved. Over the coming weeks the Government forced owners to launch an interim 'control ship', the *Ross Valiant*. Plans were drawn up for a new full-time 'mother ship' to replace the interim one. The Met. Office also placed a weather report ship in the fishing grounds. The Hull Fishing Vessels Owners' Association announced that a training ship would be set up. But the idea of having a 'shop steward' on each trawler was rejected as it might 'undermine the skipper's authority.' There were recommendations of wholesale reforms, stopping short of the 'de-casualisation' of the industry.

And in October 1968 a public inquiry was held in Hull, which resulted in the *Holland-Martin Report into Trawler Safety*. The Report was damning, saying that protective clothing could have saved the two men who perished in Eddom's lifeboat. A rubber 'duck' suit worn by Eddom, which helped save his life, was bought by him from a company store for seven guineas (£7.35).The other two had had no such clothing.

The Report also contained eighty-three safety recommendations and a demand that life rafts be equipped forthwith with safety gear. Inquiry chairman Admiral Sir Deric Holland-Martin added that the industry must *'change human attitudes at every level.'* All the demands of the *Fishermen's Charter* were enacted, most before the Inquiry, the remainder soon after.

The 'headscarf protestors' achieved in days what unions and politicians had spent decades demanding, without success. Their campaign captured the public imagination and shamed the industry and the government into immediate action.
In weeks to come some sections of the community Lillian had fought so hard to help turned on her. While Hull trawlers were subject to the bad weather ban, Icelandic trawlers continued to land fish in Hull. This even led to poison-pen letters being sent to her and her co-fighters.

After Lillian's London triumph, a TV appearance on the Eamonn Andrews Show saw her star fall with stark rapidity. During banter with the show's host, Lil was asked what fishermen did when not at sea. She quipped in her broad *'essle road* accent: *'The married ones come home and take out their wives, then go to the pubs. The single 'uns go wi' their tarts.'*

'There was an audible gasp,' recalled Mary Denness. *'In Hessle Road the word "tart" has a totally different meaning. It simply means girlfriend and is not offensive and does not have the same connotations it has elsewhere, i.e. being a prostitute.'*

Hostile letters also appeared in the local press. Skipper Len Whur, (the 'Len' appealed to in the final radio broadcast from the *Ross Cleveland*) was among her fiercest critics, accusing her of putting jobs at risk *and 'interfering in something she knew nowt about.'*

Moreover, fewer than twenty days after her Westminster trip, Lillian lost her job. While visiting students at the University of Strathclyde as a guest speaker, a letter was delivered to her home from her employers, Wilkinson Bros. (Fish Processors) of Wassand Street, Hull. In a rather haughty tone they noted she had *'not been at work for three weeks'* and therefore *'assumed she was not coming back'*–the bosses added that a week's pay was awaiting her, should she wish to pick it up.

I've been victimised says Big Lil

BIG Lil Bilocca breezed into Scotland last night . . . bristling with anger.

She claimed she had been "victimised" on being sacked from her fish cleaner's job in Hull.

Seventeen-stone Lil, touring the country on her trawler safety campaign, lashed out: "The trawler owners have pressured my bosses into sacking me because my campaign for more safety for trawlermen is costing them too much money."

Lil, 38, got her cards last Saturday from Wilkinson's Ltd.

A note from the firm's boss, Mr. Don Wilkinson, said: "Due to you not being in this last week or so we presume you have left."

Lil said:

"Well they presumed wrong and as soon as I get back home

I'm going to give them a length of my tongue.

"I went to the firm a week last Thursday and saw the boss. I told him I was going to be pretty busy until our demands for trawler safety were met.

"Personally, I couldn't care less about getting the sack. But I'm annoyed because they didn't have the courage to tell me to my face."

Last night Mr. Wilkinson said: "Mrs. Bilocca has not clocked in at our factory for three weeks.

"Naturally, we assumed she had left to carry on the work of her movement."

Today Big Lil—her husband is a merchant seaman and her son a trawlerman—will talk to students at Strathclyde University.

Mrs. Bilocca . . . a talk to students.

Fig 8.6
Glasgow Evening Times cutting kindly provided by the National Library of Scotland archive.

Mrs Bilocca never worked in fisheries again. The bosses thought her a dangerous nuisance and some of her peers thought she was 'showing up' the community. It was to be two years until she found a job. Her final job was working in the cloakroom of a Hull nightclub. In 1988, she died of cancer, aged fifty-nine. Her obituary was in *The Times*. At her funeral only a handful of those who had once cheered her no-nonsense, bluff oratory were at the graveside. She was buried alongside her beloved Charlie at Hull's Northern Cemetery, in the city's Chanterlands Avenue area.

In 1990, the local council placed a plaque on the site of the old Victoria Hall. It reads:

In recognition of the contributions to the fishing industry by the women of Hessle Road, led by Lillian Bilocca, who successfully campaigned for better safety measures following the loss of three Hull trawlers in 1968.

The 'Cod Wars'[1] led to the de-commissioning of the Hull trawler fleet, and the city's fishing industry was all but gone by 1976. Owners were compensated handsomely, while the men, deemed to be casual workers, got nothing. It was only in 2001 after a long campaign–fronted by the Hull West and Hessle MP Alan Johnson–that the then Labour Government paid compensation to the surviving trawlermen and families of those who had died in the interim.

---

1   The Cod Wars – sometimes called the Icelandic Cod Wars – were a series of disputes over fishing territories between UK and Icelandic trawlers. The first in 1958 saw the Icelanders increase their fishing territorial limit from 4 to 12 miles, in 1972 this became 50 miles and by 1975 the Icelanders had set up a 200-mile limit. Across the years there were many skirmishes between both sides but Iceland eventually achieved its aims at the expense of ports like Hull and Grimsby. For an excellent detailed account, see [6].

It is widely accepted that the direct actions of the Hessle Road Women's Committee and the courage of its leader Mrs. Lillian Bilocca saved countless lives to come and transformed forever one of the harshest, most dangerous industries on the planet.

Sources – From the PhD research of Brian Lavery BA (Hons. – 1ˢᵗ class), Dept. of English, University of Hull from his thesis 'Lillian Bilocca – The Head-Scarfed Revolutionary'.
Interviews with and acknowledgements to: Mr. Ernie Bilocca, (Lillian Bilocca's son), Mr Stuart Russell, (assistant news editor, the Hull Daily Mail, 1968-70), Lord John Prescott, (former ship's steward and union worker, later Labour politician and peer), Dr. Alec Gill, MBE, local historian and author, Mrs. Mary Denness, (trawler safety campaigner 1968), Mrs. Theresa Wade, (widow of Skipper Philip Gay of the Ross Cleveland).
Archives: The Hull Daily Mail archive housed at Hull History Centre, and also the University of Hull's Department of Maritime History archives and reference library.
Likenesses: Photo of Mrs. Lillian Bilocca (circa 1968), Commemorative plaque to Mrs. Bilocca et al, courtesy of Dr Alec Gill MBE.

References:

1. Creed, R., *Turning The Tide: The 1968 Trawler Tragedy and the Wives' Campaign for Safety, Back Door Press,* 1998.

2. Gill, A., *Superstitions: Folk Magic in Hull's Fishing Community,* Hutton Press,1993.

3. Gill, A., *Good Old Hessle Road,* Hutton Press, 1990

4. Holland-Martin, Admiral Sir Deric, *Trawler Safety: Final Report of the Committee of Inquiry into Trawler Safety, HMSO,* 1968.

5. Lavery, B.W., *Oxford Dictionary of National Biography (2013)* – entry on Mrs. Lillian Bilocca, trawler safety campaigner [1929-88]. [www.oxforddnb.com].

6. Robinson, R., *Trawling: The rise and fall of the British trawl fishery,* Exeter University Press, 1996.

7. Tunstall, J., *The Fishermen: the sociology of an extreme occupation,* McGibbon and Kee, 1962 (reprinted 1969).

Contributors

Patrick Doyle is a Durham graduate and former lecturer in History at Endsleigh College, which later merged into Humberside College of Higher Education. He served as a Hull City Councillor 1972-2002, and was Council Leader for 22 years. He is a papal Knight of St Gregory and was Provincial President of the Lay Dominicans 2007-2013.

Marie Holmes was born and raised in Hull and has worked in a variety of departments in local government, including public libraries and higher education institutions, since leaving college. She has an interest in local history and returned to education in 2003 as a very mature student, with part-time study at the University of Hull on the BA Regional and Local History programme. Graduating with an upper second-class degree in 2009, she has continued part-time study and obtained her MA in Regional and Local History and Archaeology in 2013. Currently in her first year of study, again part-time, for the PhD in History, she has a particular interest in women's history in the early 20th century. Her PhD thesis will focus on Suffrage Societies in the East Yorkshire Region.

Ekkehard Kopp is Emeritus Professor of Mathematics at Hull University, where he taught from 1970 to 2007. He has authored ten books, principally on probability theory and mathematical finance, and has served on various academic editorial boards, currently editing a series of mathematical texts for Cambridge University Press. He is Treasurer of the Hull Amnesty Group.

Brian Lavery's ongoing PhD at Hull University is in creative non-fiction, based on the Triple Trawler Disaster of 1968 and the fishwives' revolt that followed. Brian was a print and broadcast journalist for more than 25 years before returning to higher education. He is also a poet and writer of fiction. He is Mrs Lillian Bilocca's biographer and wrote the entry on her life for last year's Oxford Dictionary of National Biography. Brian also runs a community media project in east Hull. His book, *The Headscarfed Revolutionaries—Lillian Bilocca and the Hull Triple Trawler Disaster*, is due to be published by Barbican Press (www.barbicanpress.com) in Autumn 2014.

Kathleen Lennon is Professor of Philosophy at the University of Hull, and one of her specialist interests is Gender Theory. She was a founder member of the UK Society for Women and Philosophy, Hull Trades Council's Womens Committee, Hull Women's Centre and the Hull Centre for Gender Studies. She has written books and articles on, amongst other things, Self and Embodiment, Gender Theory, and the Imagination.

Cecile Oxaal is a retired secondary school teacher of English and taught in Hull for over thirty years. She is a graduate of the former University College of the West Indies (University of London), now the University of the West Indies. In 2003 she was awarded the MBE, 'for services to education in Hull'. She is the current Chair of Hull Amnesty Group.

Robb Robinson was born in Hull and is from a family engaged in the business of seafaring and fishing for generations. Based at the Maritime Historical Studies Centre, University of Hull, his numerous publications and research interests cover the fields of coastal history, fisheries and whaling in addition to the history of Hull and the Yorkshire coast. His books include *Far Horizons from Hull to the Ends of the Earth* (Hull, 2010). A Trustee of the British Commission for Maritime History, Robb worked with colleagues from various countries on the production of a two volume *History of the North Atlantic Fisheries*. He has also contributed to numerous national and regional TV and radio programmes and did the background research for, and contributed to, the *Kick Murphy Letters* programme, broadcast on Radio Humberside, which gained the national silver award in the Best Programme category at the BBC Frank Gillard Local Radio Awards in 2013. He is strongly committed to raising awareness of Hull and the East Riding's long and in many ways unique involvement with both British and world history and to using the related history and many associated success stories as a means of widening horizons.

Marion Shaw was born in Hull, brought up in the North Riding and then returned to Hull where her mother became headmistress of a junior school in the Hessle Road area. Educated at Kingston High School and then at Hull University, where for most of her academic life she was a member of the English Department. In 1993 she was appointed Professor and Head of the Department of English and Drama at Loughborough University. She retired from full-time employment in 1999, continuing on part-time contracts until 2009. Her research interests are in nineteenth-century literature and women's writing, particularly that of the interwar period. In 1972 she and two colleagues introduced the first university women's studies programme in English, and later she became the first editor of the Journal of Gender Studies.